GET SHORTY

D0755147

GET SHORTY

Screenplay by Scott Frank

Based on the novel by Elmore Leonard

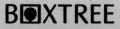

B⬛XTREE

First published in Great Britain in 1996 by Boxtree Limited,
Broadwall House, 21 Broadwall, London, SE1 9PL

GET SHORTY Copyright © 1995 by
Metro-Goldwyn-Mayer Pictures Inc

10 9 8 7 6 5 4 3 2

ISBN: 0 7522 0218 9

A CIP catalogue entry for this book is available from the British
Library

Cover design by Flash & Associates
Typeset by SX Composing DTP, Rayleigh, Essex

Printed and bound in Great Britain by
Caledonian International Book Manufacturing Ltd, Glasgow

AND . . . ACTION!

Do you want to get intimate with some of Hollywood's biggest stars? Spend a little time with them off-screen and find out how they relax, what they do for fun. Find out who they love and who they loathe, and hear the stories behind the stories of this year's blockbusters. In the past twelve months the following stars have all had leading roles in Esquire:

Robert De Niro, Nicolas Cage, Clint Eastwood, Richard Gere, Harvey Keitel, Linda Fiorentino, Tommy Lee Jones, Bruce Willis, Johnny Depp, Sharon Stone, Sylvester Stallone, Jennifer Jason Leigh, Michelle Pfeiffer, Uma Thurman, Elizabeth Hurley, Maryam d'Abo, Joely Richardson, Imogen Stubbs, Emma Thompson to name but a few . . .

Find out more about the movies with Esquire – essential reading for all film lovers every month

BLACK

MAN'S VOICE: Looks fuckin' cold out there.

EXT. VESUVIO'S RESTAURANT – MIAMI
DAY

*It is cold. People walk by hugging themselves, pulling up
their collars, etc.*

INT. VESUVIO'S RESTAURANT – SAME
TIME

*CHILI PALMER, late thirties, sits in a booth with
TOMMY CARLO, a low level mob type. Chili smokes
a cigarette, stares out the window at the people on the
street.*

TOMMY: Guy on the radio said it's gonna get
down to thirty-four.

*Chili watches a woman on the sidewalk pause to tighten
the scarf around her neck . . . She looks in the window,
sees Chili looking out.*

TOMMY: Thirty-four – that's *freezing*, for Christ
sake.

(then)

Yo, Chili, you're spacin'.

Chili turns and studies Tommy a moment, then . . .

CHILI: They're closing the Granview. You know,
theater down on Biscayne?

TOMMY: Yeah, the guy owes Momo a few G's.

CHILI: What I'm thinkin' is maybe Momo could buy it.

Tommy looks at him.

CHILI: Momo could buy it, I could run it for him. Show some Cagney films.

TOMMY: What's Momo gonna want with an old place, shows old movies people don't care about no more. Outside of maybe turnin' it into a porno house, I don't think he's gonna give much of a fuck. And you already got a job.

Chili looks back out the window again.

CHILI: Yeah.

We hear LAUGHTER O.S. and then FOCUS on the window so that Chili can now see a GROUP OF MEN reflected there, sitting at a table nearby. We hear MORE LAUGHTER and now Chili turns and looks over at . . .

RAY "BONES" BARBONI

Mob guy: tall, loud suit with lots of jewelry. As he gets up from the table, the other men around the table follow his lead as he finishes up some jokes . . .

MOB GUY: . . . so the guy says, I'm not the tailor, I'm the undertaker.

The men laugh again, more out of respect than appreciation. Ray Bones turns, sees . . .

CHILI and Tommy sitting in their booth. Tommy, sucking on a toothpick, waves.

TOMMY: Ray. How you doing?

RAY BONES: Okay, Tommy. You?

TOMMY: Okay.

Bones focuses on Chili, waits for acknowledgement. But Chili turns back to the window. Always the peacemaker, Tommy smiles at Bones again . . .

TOMMY: You believe this weather, Ray? Miami Beach, for Christ's sake.

RAY BONES: *(ignoring him)*

Chili Palmer.

(smiles)

Chilly outside. Chili inside. It's a regular fuckin' chili-fest. Hey, waiter – give Mr. Chili Pepper a big fuckin' bowl of chili!

Again the men all laugh respectfully at Ray Bone's stupid joke. Chili smiles the best he can at the idiot . . .

CHILI: Good to see you, Ray.

He turns back to the window, watches Ray Bones in the reflection, still cracking up as he and his men head for the front of the restaurant. Tommy looks at Chili for a moment, then stands up . . .

TOMMY: You done starin' out the window, I'll see you back at the office.

Chili nods, but still doesn't turn from the window. He merely watches in the glass as Tommy turns up his collar and steps out into the cold Miami day.

TOMMY: *Jesus.* It's freezin'!

Chili then puts out the cigarette, nods to the waiter who comes over with the check.

INT. RESTAURANT COATROOM – A FEW MINUTES LATER

From inside the tiny room. A couple of ratty rain coats and an old flight jacket hang to one side in immediate f.g. as Chili steps into the doorway and freezes. He looks o.s. and whistles . . .

CHILI: Hey.

A moment later the MANAGER, an old Italian guy in a black suit, joins him in the doorway.

CHILI: What happened to my coat?

The Manager peers into the room . . .

MANAGER: It's not one of these?

CHILI: You see a black leather jacket, fingertip length, like the one Pacino wore in *Serpico?* You don't, you owe me three seventy-nine.

MANAGER: Maybe you don't see my sign?

The manager points to a sign on the wall: 'WE CANNOT BE RESPONSIBLE FOR LOST ARTICLES.'

CHILI: Look, I didn't come down to sunny Florida to freeze my ass. You follow me? You get the coat back or you give me the three seventy-nine my ex-wife paid for it at Alexander's.

The Manager looks o.s., and begins speaking in Italian. Chili reacts as we hear the name RAY BARBONI mentioned a couple of times.

MANAGER: Explain to him how Mr. Barboni borrow the coat.

A WAITER joins Chili and the Manager in the doorway.

CHILI: Ray Bones took my coat? Just now?

WAITER: He didn't *take* it. He *borrow* it. See, someone took *his* coat, you know . . . (*indicates flight jacket*) . . . leave this old one. So Mr. Barboni, he put on this *other* coat that fit him pretty good.

CHILI: You mean *my* coat.

WAITER: He was wearing it, you know, to go home. He wasn't gonna keep it.

CHILI: My car keys were in that coat.

MANAGER: We call you a taxi.

CHILI: Lemme get this straight. You aren't responsible for any lost articles like an expensive coat of mine, but you're gonna find Ray Bones' coat or get him a new one? Is that what you're telling me?

MANAGER: Mr. Barboni a good customer.

(*making sure to add*)

Works for Jimmy Capp.

CHILI: I know who he works for. Where's your phone.

INT. TOMMY CARLO'S CAR – DAY

Tommy drives. Chili stares straight ahead, rubs his hands together, tries to stay warm . . .

TOMMY: You sure it was Ray Bones took the coat?

CHILI: That's what the guy said.

TOMMY: *(nervous now)* Tomorrow, I see on the TV weather, it's gonna be nice and warm. You won't need the coat.

Chili points out the window.

CHILI: This is it.

EXT. VICTOR HOTEL – DAY

As Tommy pulls up out front.

INT. CAR – SAME TIME

Tommy looks up at the hotel as Chili takes a pair of leather gloves from top of the dash, opens the door. Tommy looks over at him.

TOMMY: Hey, Chili,

(Chili pauses)

Get your coat, but don't piss the guy off, okay? It could get complicated and we'd have to call Momo to straighten it out. Then Momo gets pissed for wasting his time and we don't need that.

CHILI: Don't worry about it. I won't say any more than I have to, if that.

EXT. STAIRS – DAY

Chili pulls on the gloves as he goes up the stairs to the third floor.

EXT. DOOR – DAY

As Chili knocks on the door three times. He waits, pulls the right-hand glove on tight, so that when . . .

RAY BONES opens the door, Chili nails him. One punch. No need to throw the left.

RAY BONES: Jesus . . . Oh, God . . .

Chili then steps over him into the room and grabs his coat from a chair. He looks over at Ray Bones bent over, blood running from his nose and mouth, blood all over his hands, his shirt.

RAY BONES: Fuck, man . . .

Chili walks out. Doesn't say one word to Ray Bones.

EXT. BARBER SHOP – DAY

A warmer day. The sun is shining. All is quiet.

INT. BARBER SHOP – SAME TIME

The place is empty except for FRED and ED, the two old barbers sitting in the chairs, reading newspapers.

ED: You been there, haven't you?

INT. BARBER SHOP BACKROOM – SAME TIME

A room Tommy and Chili use as an office. Chili sits at the desk making entries in the collection book. We can hear the two old barbers talking o.s. . . .

FRED: *(O.S.)* Paris? Yeah, I been there plenty times. It's right offa Seventy-nine.

ED: *(O.S.)* Hell it is. It's on Sixty-eight. Seventeen miles from Lexington.

FRED: *(O.S.)* What're you talking about, Paris, Kentucky, or Paris, Tennessee?

Silence. No answer to the question. Chili look up from the collection book, listens a moment to nothing.

He opens the desk drawer and pulls out a .38. He aims the gun at the open doorway . . .

OVER CHILI'S SHOULDER

As Ray Bones, a bandage on his nose, appears in the back hall, then the doorway to the office, his face showing surprise to see a gun aimed at him . . .

Ray Bones begins firing the big Colt auto in his hand, maybe before he's ready, the gun making an awful racket, when Chili pulls the trigger, shooting Ray Bones along the top of his head, creasing him from hairline to crown.

Chili calmly gets to his feet. Aims once more – probably lower this time – but doesn't fire as Ray Bones grabs his head and stumbles out of there.

RAY BONES: *(O.S.)* Somebody call 9 fucking 111.

EXT. MIAMI HARBOR – DAY

Ray Bones, a bandage on his head now as well as his nose, sits on a cigarette boat with his boss, JIMMY CAP and two bikini clad BABES, both of whom rub lotion on Jimmy.

JIMMY: Whatta you want me to do Ray? Go to war over a fuckin *coat*? You're lucky the guy didn't kill you. The coat was a Christmas present for Christ's sake.

RAY BONES: You gotta do *somethin'*, Jimmy. This man's got no respect for us.

JIMMY: He's got no respect for *you*, and I don't gotta do shit. Chili Palmer don't work for me, he works for Momo up in Brooklyn. So as long as Momo's around, nothing happens to Chili Palmer. You understand?

As an angry Ray Bones sits back, we . . .

FADE TO BLACK

EXT. BROOKLYN STREET – NIGHT

We TILT DOWN to REVEAL a dark Brooklyn street as a black Cadillac pulls to a stop in front of an older building.

VOICE: Momo. We're here.

Two big guys, BODYGUARDS, get out of the car. One of them opens the back door for a huge man, MOMO, who gets out of the car and looks up at the dark building . . .

MOMO: You check this place out good? If I'm going up alone, I don't want no surprises.

BODYGUARD: I checked it out, boss.

INT. BROOKLYN TENEMENT BUILDING – NIGHT

Momo eyes the bodyguards – both nervous – then starts up the steps. We follow Momo as he enters the building, goes up the dark stairwell . . . up one flight . . . we're behind him the whole time . . .

When he gets to the top floor, Momo pauses to catch his breath, before moving on down the hall to a door. Momo knocks.

VOICE: Yeah?

MOMO: It's Momo.

VOICE: Come in.

Momo slowly opens the door . . . when, suddenly, the apartment is FLOODED WITH LIGHT so that we see a room full of PEOPLE, a banner on the back wall reading 'HAPPY SIXTY-FIFTH, MOMO!'

EVERYONE: Surprise!

Silence as Momo drops to his knees, gurgles something we can't understand and falls over. Suddenly a dozen faces are looking down on us as we then . . .

CUT TO: EXT. BARBER SHOP – DAY

A beautiful day in Miami.

CHILI: *(V.O.)* So what're you tellin' me, you're never gonna go to sleep again?

INT. BARBER SHOP – DAY

Chili and Tommy each sit in a barber chair, reading the newspaper while Fred and Ed sit nearby playing checkers.

TOMMY: No, I said I'm never goin' to bed. There's a difference. See, the article says most people die in their beds. I figure long as I stay outta bed, I'm safe.

CHILI: That's the dumbest thing I ever heard. Where do you sleep?

TOMMY: In an armchair. Or I go to a coffee shop, sleep there. Sit in a booth, pull my hat down.

A car pulls up. Chili's no longer listening to Tommy, but now watching as Ray Bones and a BLACK GUY get out of the car.

TOMMY: How many people you hear ever die in a coffee shop?

Tommy looks over as Ray Bones – smaller bandage on the top of his head – and his man enter the shop.

RAY BONES: You cut straight hair in this place, or just fags?

CHILI: Hey, Bones, looks like you're gonna have a nice scar up there. Maybe these guys can fit you with a rug, cover it up for ya.

Ray Bones eyes Chili, then nods to Fred and Ed.

RAY BONES: Why don't you geezers take your game over to the park.

The two guys leave as the Black Guy steps up to Chili . . .

BLACK GUY: This man is the man, you understand what I'm saying? He's *Mr.* Bones, you speak to him from now on.

Chili exchanges a look with Tommy, watches as 'Mr. Bones' goes down the hall into the back office, then turns to the black guy . . .

CHILI: You can do better'n him.

BLACK GUY: Not these days. Not less you can talk Spanish.

Ray Bones comes out with the collection book open, looking at all of the names of who owes what.

RAY BONES: You got a miss. Leo Devoe. Guy's six weeks over.

CHILI: He died.

RAY BONES: How'd you know he died, he tell you?

Ray Bones checks his man to get some appreciation, but the guy's too busy looking at the hair rinses and shit on the counter.

CHILI: Yeah, he told me.

RAY BONES: Personally?

CHILI: Yeah, Ray, he personally told me he got killed in that Get Away Airlines' jet went down last month.

RAY BONES: What Get Away jet?

CHILI: It was in the *Herald.*

RAY BONES: Yeah, well, maybe the guy took out flight insurance. Check with the wife.

CHILI: Hey, it's your book now. You want to check it out, go ahead. He's got a dry cleaning business out on Federal Highway.

Tommy gives Chili a look as the Black Guy comes over to Chili, stands next to him. Ray Bones steps over to Chili . . .

RAY BONES: Momo's dead. Which means anything was his now belongs to Jimmy Capp, including *you.*

Tommy watches as the Black Guy picks up a pair of scissors, runs his hand along the edge . . .

RAY BONES: Which also means when I speak, I'm speakin' for Jimmy. So e.g. as of now, you start affording me the proper respect.

CHILI: 'e.g.' means 'for example', Ray. I think what you wanna say is 'i.e.'

RAY BONES: Bullshit. E.g. is short for 'ergo'.

CHILI: Ask your man here.

Ray Bones looks at the Black Guy.

BLACK GUY: Best a my knowledge, e.g. means 'for example.'

RAY BONES: e.g., i.e., fuck you. The point is, I say jump, you say okay. Okay?

TOMMY: *(for Chili)* Yeah, Ray. Okay.

Ray Bones then nods to his man who grabs Chili, holds the point of the scissors to Chili's throat . . .

RAY BONES: You owe me the dry cleaner's fifteen grand plus the juice which is what another, uhh . . .

CHILI: Twenty seven hundred.

RAY BONES: Exactly. You either get it from the wife or out of your own pocket, I don't give a fuck. You don't ever hand me a book with a miss in it.

Ray throws the book at Chili and walks out, his man right behind him. Chili looks over at Tommy.

TOMMY: I told you not to –

CHILI: Don't say a fuckin' word.

EXT. FAY DEVOE'S BACKYARD – DUSK

Where Chili sits with FAY DEVOE – thirties, attractive, in a sundress – on her patio. They each have a drink . . .

FAY: I hate the dry cleaning business. I hate being inside all day, around all those machines.

CHILI: Must be hot.

FAY: You have no idea how hot it is.

She looks at him. Touches her drink to the side of her face. Chili finishes his drink, sets it down.

CHILI: I was wondering, Fay, if Leo had any life insurance.

FAY: I don't know of any.

They sit there in silence a moment. Fay reaches over, puts a hand on his leg . . .

FAY: I trust you, Chili. I think you're a decent type of man, even if you are a crook.

CHILI: Thank you Fay.

She finally looks at Chili . . .

FAY: I wish he really was dead, the son of a bitch.

EXT. LAS VEGAS – NIGHT

The strip. Mesas Casino.

CUT TO: CLOSE UP OF PHOTOGRAPH

Leo Devoe. Standing with Fay at Epcot Center.

DICK: *(V.O.)* That's him all right.

PULL BACK TO REVEAL INT. DICK ALLEN'S OFFICE – NIGHT

*A sign on the door reads "DICK ALLEN,
CUSTOMER RELATIONS." A bank of video
monitors show the floor of the casino. Chili sits across the
desk from DICK ALLEN – lots of jewelry, a giant
NEON COWGIRL out the window behind him.*

DICK: Called himself Larry DeMille. Hit on every
showgirl in town. Would tell 'em he was the
'Martinizing King of Miami'. What a moron.

He returns the snapshot to Chili.

DICK: Anyway, you want this guy, he's in L.A.
We put him on a flight after he spanked one a my
cocktail girls in the Keno room.

CHILI: Leo spanked a waitress?

DICK: Apparently, way it went, he invited her to
come to Santa Anita to play the ponies with him.
She told him what to do with that and he gave her
one on the tush. My guess, he's by his lonesome at
the track right now.

Chili nods.

DICK: Hey, Chil? Since you're goin' out to L.A.
anyway.

CHILI: What've you got?

DICK: Guy owes us a hundred and fifty grand,
sixty days over; a movie producer.

CHILI: Movie producer? Yeah, why not.

As Dick Allen reaches for a pad of paper, we hear THE

SOUND OF AN AIRPLANE OVER . . .

EXT.LAX RENTAL CAR LOT – NIGHT

It's raining as we TILT DOWN from a LANDING AIRPLANE to a National Car Rental BUS arriving next to a tan MINIVAN. Chili eyes the car a moment, then turns to the driver.

CHILI: What is this?

ATTENDANT: An Oldsmobile Silhouette.

CHILI: I reserved a Cadillac.

ATTENDANT: Yeah, well, this one's the Cadillac of minivans.

CHILI: You're kidding me, right?

ATTENDANT: Hey, you want La Tierra Rent-A-Car just over there, but I think all they got are Rabbit convertibles.

Chili gives the driver a look then gets out of the bus, standing there in the rain, his suit getting wet, nowhere to go. He turns and stares at the minivan . . .

EXT. KAREN FLORES' HOUSE – NIGHT

All the lights are out, save the BLUE GLOW of a television coming from one of the downstairs rooms . . .

WOMAN'S VOICE: *(loud whisper)* Harry?

INT. KAREN FLORES' BEDROOM – NIGHT

As KAREN FLORES, pretty, endowed, sits up in bed wearing a Lakers T-shirt, nothing else. She looks at the big shape lying under the covers beside her.

KAREN: *Harry.*

The shape doesn't move. She shakes it.

KAREN: Harry, God damn it, somebody's downstairs.

The shape stirs, rolls over, and we see HARRY ZIMM, balding, overweight; a movie producer. He sits up.

HARRY: What's wrong?

KAREN: Be quiet and listen.

HARRY: I don't hear anything.

We hear VOICES downstairs.

KAREN: Shhh – *there.*

And now LAUGHTER . . .

HARRY: Sounds like the television.

She looks at him . . .

KAREN: When I came upstairs, you stayed to finish your drink. I told you to turn off the TV when you were through.

(an afterthought)

Come to think of it, I also told you you could sleep in the maid's room.

HARRY: Yeah, well I turned off the set. I used the remote control thing and laid it on the floor. You know what could've happened? The dog came in and stepped on it, turned the TV back on.

KAREN: I don't have a dog.

HARRY: You don't? What happened to Muff?

KAREN: Harry, are you going down, or you want me to?

He grunts, gets out of bed. Starts looking around the room for his clothes. Harry looks out the window . . .

HARRY: Anyone skim the pool? It needs it.

KAREN: Harry –

HARRY: I'm going.

INT. HALLWAY – SAME TIME

The MONOTONE VOICES become louder and more distinct as Harry moves down the curved staircase in his shirt and boxer shorts. One of the voices is familiar . . .

We can see this is a nice place as Harry crosses the entry hall to a doorway, the FLICKERING LIGHT of the television emitting from inside the room.

Harry listens at the door. Yeah, it's David Letterman.

INT. KAREN'S STUDY – SAME TIME

Harry moves into the glow of the big Sony, the rest of the room dark. On the tube, Dave is interviewing actor Martin Weir when suddenly the screen goes black and the desk lamp comes on. Harry jumps . . .

HARRY: Jesus Christ!

Chili leans into the light, keeps his tone quiet, controlled.

CHILI: Harry Zimm, how you doing? I'm Chili Palmer.

Harry presses a hand against his chest.

HARRY: Jesus, if I have a heart attack, I hope you know what to do.

CHILI: Where you been, Harry?

Harry lets his hand slide down over his belly, taking his time, wanting to show that he has it together now.

HARRY: Have we met? I don't recall.

CHILI: We just did. I told you my name's Chili Palmer.

Harry stares back, trying to figure out who this guy is.

HARRY: You're in pictures, right?

Chili smiles. Doesn't say anything.

HARRY: Did you stop to think what if I had a heart attack?

CHILI: You look okay to me, Harry. Come over here and sit down. Tell me what you been up to.

Harry takes one of the canvas director's chairs by the desk. He looks at a bottle of Dewars sitting there, runs a hand through his hair, thinks about a drink . . .

CHILI: Harry, look at me.

Harry brings his hand down.

HARRY: I'm looking at you.

CHILI: I want you to keep looking right here, okay?

HARRY: That's what I'm doing.

CHILI: You know Dick Allen, Mesa's Casino?

HARRY: Dick Allen's a very dear friend of mine. How far you want to go with this?

CHILI: We're there, Harry. You signed markers for a hundred and a half, you're over sixty days past due and you haven't told anybody what the problem is.

Harry looks at Chili.

HARRY: Jesus Christ, what're you, a collector for a fucking casino? You come in here, walk in the house in the middle of the fucking night? I thought you were an actor, *auditioning*, for Christ's sake.

Chili nods, almost smiles . . .

CHILI: Is that right? That's interesting. You thought I was acting, huh?

Harry pushes out of the chair, looks down at Chili.

HARRY: We'll see about this . .

Harry grabs the phone, punches the 'O'.

HARRY: Operator, how do I get Las Vegas Information?

CHILI: Harry, lemme give you some advice.

Chili leans forward, hangs up the phone with his index finger, casually reaches for the receiver . . .

CHILI: You don't want to act like a hard-on, you're standing there in your undies. You know what I'm saying? What you want to do is sit down and talk to me.

Harry sits down. Chili hangs up the phone.

CHILI: A marker's like a check, Harry.

HARRY: I know what a marker is.

CHILI: They don't want to deposit yours and have it bounce. That annoys them. So your dear friend Dick Allen's been calling, leaving messages on your machine, but you never get back to him. I happen to be in Vegas on another matter, and Dick asks me as a favor would I look you up. I follow you over here, see you in the window with this woman, looks a lot like that actress Karen Flores, was in *Grotesque,* except she's not blond anymore . . .

Harry's gaze moves to the bottle of scotch on the desk . . .

CHILI: You're not looking at me, Harry.

HARRY: Why do I have to keep looking at you?

CHILI: I want you to.

HARRY: You gonna get rough now, threaten me? I make good by tomorrow or get my legs broken?

CHILI: Come on, Harry – Mesas? The worst they might do is get a judgment against you, uttering a bad check. I can't imagine you want that to happen, man in your position.

HARRY: Fuckin' basketball game.

Harry reaches for the bottle of scotch and pours himself a drink.

HARRY: Tell Dick Allen I'll cover the markers in the next sixty days at the most. He doesn't like it, that's his problem. The prick.

Harry starts to take another drink, looks at Chili, not moving.

HARRY: So, you want me to call you a cab?

Chili shakes his head, keeps staring at Harry, but with a different expression now, more thoughtful, curious . . .

CHILI: You make movies, huh?

HARRY: I produce feature motion pictures, no TV. You mentioned *Grotesque*, that happened to be *Grotesque Part II* that Karen Flores was in. She starred in all three of my *Slime Creatures* releases you might have seen.

Chili nods, leans forward on the desk.

CHILI: I think I got an idea for a movie.

INT. KAREN FLORES' BEDROOM – NIGHT

Karen is sitting up in bed, listening. We hear the muffled sounds of Chili and Harry talking downstairs. She gets out of bed . . .

INT. HALLWAY – SAME TIME

Chili and Harry's conversation gets louder as Karen descends the stairs. She peers into the study, but they're not in there . . .

INT. KITCHEN – SAME TIME

Chili sits with Harry at a butcher block table, a bottle of Dewars and a couple of glasses now between them.

CHILI: Yeah, Leo wore these little plaid hats – Miami, middle of the summer, this guy thinks no one's gonna notice he's balding, he wears a fuckin' hat.

Harry looks up past Chili, smiles.

HARRY: Karen?

Chili turns around and sees her standing in the doorway now, her arms folded across that chest; the Lakers T-shirt coming down just past her crotch.

HARRY: Karen, say hello to Chili Palmer. Chili, this is Karen Flores.

CHILI: Karen, it's a pleasure. How you doing?

KAREN: How did you get in the house?

HARRY: He's telling me an idea for a movie. It's not bad so far.

(motions with his glass)

Sit down, have a drink.

(to Chili)

Tell Karen, let's see what she thinks.

KAREN: Maybe you didn't hear me.

CHILI: The door from the patio, in back.

KAREN: You broke in?

CHILI: No, it was open. It wasn't locked.

KAREN: What if it was?

Chili doesn't say anything, just watches her, likes the way she's handling it.

HARRY: You want to hear this idea? It's about a dry cleaner who scams an airline out of three hundred grand. Go on, tell her.

CHILI: You just did.

HARRY: I mean, the way you told it to me. Start at the beginning, we see how the story line develops.

Chili looks at Karen. She leans in the doorway.

CHILI: Well, basically, this guy owes a shylock fifteen thousand, plus he's a few weeks behind on the vig, the interest you have to pay.

KAREN: I know what a vig is.

HARRY: It's the kind of situation, you don't pay, you get your legs broken.

CHILI: Or the guy *thinks* he could get 'em broken. You have to understand the loan shark's in business the same as anybody else. He isn't in it to hurt people. He's in it to make money.

EXT. LEO DEVOE'S HOUSE – DAY

As we see Chili talking to Fay on the front porch.

CHILI: *(V.O.)* But the dry cleaner, we'll call him Leo, he's scared, doesn't know any better, so he takes off –

INT. KAREN'S KITCHEN – NIGHT

As Harry jumps in . . .

HARRY: That's Miami. He's going to Vegas. He's got a few bucks and he's thinking it's his only chance.

INT. AIRPLANE – DAY

We see a fidgety LEO DEVOE, a little guy in a crummy suit and a little green hat sitting there in coach, looking around.

CHILI: *(V.O.)* Leo gets on a plane, ready to go, but the plane sits there at the gate, doesn't move.

Behind Leo sits a BRAT with his MOM and DAD. The parents are trying to entertain the kid with the G.I. Joes, other stuff they've brought along, but the kid spots Leo's hat as Leo looks up to listen to an announcement . . .

CHILI: *(V.O.)* They announce over the PA there's some kind of mechanical problem, they'll be there maybe an hour, but keep your seats in case they get it fixed sooner.

Leo gets really uncomfortable now . . .

CHILI: *(V.O.)* The guy's nervous, in no shape to just sit there, sweat it out. So he gets off the plane . . .

As Leo gets up from his seat, the kids knocks off Leo's little green hat, and we . . .

CUT TO: INT. MIAMI AIRPORT COCKTAIL LOUNGE – DAY

As Leo downs a drink, looks around for the waitress . . .

CHILI: *(V.O.)* Goes in the cocktail lounge and starts throwing 'em down, one after the other.

He's motioning to her for another, when we see a PLANE taxi past the window in the b.g. . . .

CHILI: *(V.O.)* When the plane pulls away from the gate.

INT. KAREN'S KITCHEN – NIGHT

As Harry interrupts.

HARRY: *Without* him. The guy's so out of it he doesn't even know it's gone.

CHILI: That's right. As a matter of fact . . .

INT. COCKTAIL LOUNGE – DAY

A shit-faced Leo struggles to keep his head up as he watches the waitress look out the window and gasp . . .

CHILI: *(V.O.)* He's *still* in the lounge when a plane blows up on the runway . . .

We see a BIG FIREBALL in the b.g. as Leo's head hits the table.

INT. KAREN'S KITCHEN – NIGHT

As Chili lights a cigarette.

CHILI: So when the guy finds out it was his flight, he can't believe it. If he'd stayed on that plane, he'd be dead. Right then he knows his luck has changed. If everybody thinks he's dead he won't have to pay back the fifteen or what he owes on the vig, four and a half a week.

Chili offers the pack to Karen. Karen doesn't move.

KAREN: The interest is four hundred and fifty dollars a week on fifteen thousand?

CHILI: That's right. Three percent.

KAREN: But a week. That's a hundred and fifty percent a year.

CHILI: A hundred and fifty-six. Some'll charge you more'n that, go as high as six for five on a short-term loan. So three a week's not too bad.

KAREN: A real bargain.

She shakes her head, keeps her arms folded. Chili watches her, likes the way she's giving it to him.

HARRY: Keep going.

CHILI: Well, since Leo's name was on the passenger list . . .

INT. AIRPORT HANGER – DAY

As an FFA OFFICIAL leads Fay, a black veil over her face, amongst tables full of charred items . . .

CHILI: *(V.O.)* They bring his wife out to the airport where they're going through personal effects, whatever wasn't burned up. Leo's bags were on the plane, so the wife tells 'em what to look for, things only she would know about.

FAY REACTS as the FFA guy points to a LITTLE GREEN HAT on one of the tables. She grabs it, clutches it to her chest, pretends to faint.

INT. KAREN'S KITCHEN – NIGHT

As Karen finds herself listening, despite herself.

CHILI: A couple days ago by, people from the airliner come to see his wife, tell her how sorry they are and all that their plane exploded and offer her a settlement, the amount based on what he would've earned operating the dry cleaner's the rest of his life. Leo had some kind of trouble with his kidneys, so they were giving him about ten years.

KAREN: How much is the wife offered?

Chili starts to speak, but Harry cuts him off.

HARRY: Three hundred grand, and they take it, money in hand, babe. The guy has his wife cash the check and he takes off for Las Vegas with the dough. Gets there, he's supposed to call her, tell her when to come out. But she never hears from him again.

Meanwhile, the guy's hot, runs the three hundred up to half a million . . .

CHILI: He comes to L. A. . . .

Harry raises his hand to stop Chili. He's rolling, turns to Karen now . . .

HARRY: It drives the guy nuts, he's winning but can't tell anybody who he is. You show in a back story his motivation, his desire to be famous, you know, pal around with celebrities, the headliners doing the big rooms. Now he's got the dough to buy his way in, mix with celebs and he can't resist . . .

Harry then turns back to Chili.

HARRY: So he comes to L. A. . . .

CHILI: I don't know about his wanting to meet celebrities, that's something new. But, yeah, he comes to L. A. Then after that, I don't know what happens.

Chili looks at Karen. Patient. Not moving.

HARRY: That's it? That's your movie?

CHILI: I said I had an idea, that's all.

HARRY: That's half a movie, with holes in it. Maybe forty minutes of screen time. You don't even have a girl, a female lead, and on top of that, there's no one to sympathize with, you don't have a good guy.

CHILI: The shylock's the good guy.

HARRY: The shylock? He's barely mentioned. And it's not believable the wife would get a settlement that fast.

KAREN: Harry doesn't realize it's a true story.

They both look at her now.

KAREN: That Miami flight that went down, it was on the news every day for about a week. Harry must've been busy.

HARRY: That's where you got the idea?

CHILI: Part of it, yeah.

HARRY: Wait a minute, you're not the guy, are you? The dry cleaner?

CHILI: You mean, Leo?

HARRY: You wouldn't be talking to me if you were.

CHILI: I'm not the guy, Harry.

HARRY: But you work for the casino?

CHILI: I'm out here looking for Leo. I just looked you up as a favor to your dear friend, Dick Allen.

HARRY: So you *don't* work for the casino?

KAREN: Harry, for God's sake . . .

They both look at her.

KAREN: He's the shylock.

She's staring at Chili again. Harry turns to him.

HARRY: Is that right, that's what you do for a living?

CHILI: What I did till recently.

(looking at Karen)

After I get done here I'll think about what I'm gonna do next.

KAREN: With your experience, you could always become an agent. Right, Harry?

HARRY: Yeah, that's what we need. More agents.

KAREN: Well. I got an audition tomorrow.

HARRY: No problem. You go on off to bed.

Karen looks at the two of them sitting there. Not about to move.

KAREN: What I'm saying, Harry, is I want you and your new buddy to get out of my house.

HARRY: Oh, yeah, sure.

CHILI: Nice meeting you, Karen.

She just looks at him, turns and walks out. Chili watches her go. Harry watches Chili, pours the last of the scotch into Chili's glass . . .

HARRY: I imagine in your line of work, there were times you had to get rough, you know, say one of your customers stopped paying.

CHILI: They always paid.

Harry nods, thinks a moment, then . . .

HARRY: You pack a gun?

CHILI: Not really.

HARRY: What does that mean?

CHILI: Maybe a few times I have.

HARRY: Ever shot anybody.

CHILI: Once.

HARRY: Really? You ever been arrested?

CHILI: I've been picked up a couple times. Loan sharking. Racketeering. But I was never convicted. I'm clean.

HARRY: Racketeering, that covers a lot of ground, doesn't it?

Chili looks at him.

CHILI: Why don't you get to the point, Harry? You want me to do something for you.

EXT. FAY DEVOE'S HOUSE – MORNING

As a Cadillac Eldorado pulls up out front and Ray Bones and his man get out, check out the neighborhood . . .

RAY BONES: Hi, I'm Ray, a friend of Chili Palmer's.

INT. FAY DEVOE'S HOUSE – MORNING.

Fay watches as Ray Bones and his man go through her things.

RAY BONES: Have your spoken to Mr. Palmer since your husband . . . you know, blew up?

FAY: Maybe once or twice.

RAY BONES: *(coming over)* What was it you talked about?

FAY: Oh, nothing really? This and that.

Ray Bones hits Fay Devoe in the face. She drops to her knees and cries out. Ray Bones crouches down in front of her, puts a hand in her hair.

RAY BONES: Fay . . .

(pulls her head up)

Fay.

She looks at him. Afraid now, her nose is bleeding. Ray Bones smiles at her, strokes her hair.

RAY BONES: Fay, I want us to be friends. And friends don't hit each other, 'less they have to.

(she nods)

So whatta you say we start all over and you tell me exactly what the fuck is goin' on?

EXT. SUNSET BOULEVARD – MORNING

As we BOOM DOWN from a massive billboard for the movie Bonaparte *starring Martin Weir as Napoleon and begin tracking with Harry's eight-year-old, battered*

Mercedes . . .

INT. HARRY'S CAR – SAME TIME

Harry drives, all the while gesturing with a lit cigarette.

HARRY: These guys, my investors, they run a limo service, came to me originally, put money in a few of my pictures and did okay, they're happy. So they come in on another deal – this was back a few months ago when I was planning what would be my next picture, about this band of killer circus freaks that travel around the country leaving bodies in their wake. The characters, there's this seven-hundred-pound fat lady who has a way of seducing guys, gets them in her trailer –

CHILI: Harry, look at me.

Harry looks at him. Chili takes away his cigarette.

CHILI: You're trying to tell me how you fucked up without sounding stupid, and that's hard to do. Let's just get to where you're at, okay? You blew the two hundred grand the limo guys gave you in Vegas on a basketball game and you haven't told 'em about it. Why not?

HARRY: Because they're not the type of guys would take it with any degree of understanding or restraint. The first thing they'd do is break my legs.

CHILI: You got that on the brain, Harry. If you're so scared of 'em why'd you take their money to Vegas to begin with?

HARRY: Because I need half a million to buy a script.

CHILI: For a movie?

HARRY: A blockbuster. But *quality*. No mutants or maniacs. This one's gonna be my *Driving Miss Daisy*.

CHILI: What's it called?

HARRY: *Mr. Lovejoy*.

CHILI: *Mr. Lovejoy*? That's the title?

HARRY: It's not bad when you know what it's about.

Harry pulls to the curb, faces Chili . . .

HARRY: Murray Saffrin, guy who wrote it, did all my *Grotesque* pictures, had it in a drawer for twenty years. He shows it to me one day, tells me he's got a star interested, would I produce it.

CHILI: Who's the star?

Harry points across the street to the Cafe Med where we see a RED FERRARI convertible parked out the front. We see MARTIN WEIR and a WOMAN with jet-black hair sitting at a table . . .

HARRY: Two time academy award nominee, Martin Weir.

CHILI: Martin Weir. He played the mob guy that turned snitch in *The Cyclone*.

HARRY: One of his best parts.

CHILI: No, his best part was the cripple gay guy that climbed Mt. Whitney.

HARRY: *Ride the Clouds*. Good picture.

They watch Martin and the girl a moment . . .

CHILI: She looks familiar.

HARRY: She's a rock star. Every day, same time, they come down here and have breakfast. He has the egg white omelette; she has the banana pancakes. He sits facing west so he can see his billboard. She faces east so she has an excuse to wear the shades.

Harry pulls out, starts driving again . . .

HARRY: Anyway, Murray has this shrink, who also happens to be Martin's personal trainer's shrink. Murray gives the shrink the script and the shrink gives it to Martin's trainer who reads it to Martin while they work out, and Martin flips. Loves it.

CHILI: So what's the problem?

HARRY: The problem is Murray. He and a few other blocked screenwriters went river rafting down the Kern a few weeks ago. Murray never made it back.

CHILI: He drown?

HARRY: Heart attack. Apparently they brought a couple hookers along.

Chili nods, looks up at an ANGELYNE billboard . . .

HARRY: Doris, Murray's widow, finds out about this Martin Weir thing and says since Murray and I never had any written contract, she wants five hundred grand for the script.

CHILI: So you're thinking what if I was to put you next to my dry cleaner. Ask him if he wants to invest his money in a movie.

HARRY: That, or I'm thinking what if some tragic accident were to befall the widow Saffrin –

CHILI: I'm not gonna pop her, Harry.

HARRY: Just a thought.

CHILI: But I could talk to the limo guys. Tell 'em to leave you alone for a while. Make the point in a way they'd understand it.

HARRY: You don't even know these guys.

CHILI: Harry, I probably know 'em better than you do.

HARRY: What do you get out of this?

CHILI: Let's see how we get along.

EXT. PARKING LOT – DAY

BO CATLETT, black, tall, put together in a tan outfit: suit, shirt, tie, lies on the hood of a BLACK STRETCH LIMO, his back against the windshield, reading Daily Variety, *a headline proclaiming* 'BONAPARTE STANDS TALL AT THE B. O.' *We hear the sound of an AIRPLANE and he checks his watch.*

He casually folds the newspaper as a 747 screams past directly overhead and we . . .

PULL BACK TO REVEAL: LAX – DAY

As Bo Catlett pounds twice on the fender . . .

BO CATLETT: That's us.

INT. SOVEREIGN TERMINAL – DAY

Bo Catlett walks through the terminal. We hear the arrival of the Miami flight announced over the PA as Catlett stops at one of the gates.

We see a plane pulling into the gate through the glass as Bo Catlett checks out the other people waiting to greet the flight . . .

Like, for example, the YOUNG DUDE in jeans and a wool shirt hanging out.

Bo Catlett studies him a moment, then sits down in one of the chairs. He looks over at . . .

A BIG MAN, bearded, wearing a loud Hawaiian shirt, and carrying a three-year-old GIRL in his arms. The girl licks an ice-cream, spilling some on Daddy's shirt . . .

Bo Catlett looks over as disembarking PASSENGERS start coming through the gate.

As a LATINO MAN gets off the plane and glances around. He looks uncomfortable in the loose-fitting suit, like a migrant dressed for Saturday night.

*The Latino Man lays his TICKET ENVELOPE on
top of the trash container near the gateway . . .*

INSERT – TICKET ENVELOPE

*The name Y. PORTILLO printed on the outside. The
big man with the little girl picks up the ticket and walks
away.*

As the LATINO MAN

heads straight for Bo Catlett.

BO CATLETT: Don't say nothing to me. Sit
down and act like you're waiting for somebody
supposed to meet you.

LATINO MAN: The fock you taking about . . .

Hitting the word hard, like Tony Montana in Scarface.

LATINO MAN: They nobody know me here,
man. Give me the focking money.

BO CATLETT: *Sit down.* Now be *look*ing. Man
over to your right in the blue wool shirt hanging
out . . . the other way, *derecho* . . .

*Bo Catlett hunches over to rest his arms on his thighs, so
that the Latino Man is now between him and the dude in
the wool shirt.*

BO CATLETT: That's a federal officer, most
likely DEA. He moves his leg look for the bulge.
You savvy bulge? That's his backup piece . . . *Hey.*
Try it without looking right at him if you can.

The Latino Man, trying to be cool about it, checks out the dude in the wool shirt. Sure enough, there's a bulge down near the guy's ankle.

BO CATLETT: What's your name?

LATINO MAN: *(nervous now)* Yayo. Portillo.

BO CATLETT: Alright, Yayo, you know he's there, now forget about him. Now I'm gonna get up. Soon as I'm gone, you sit down in this same seat I'm in. You feel something under your ass it's the key to a locker where your half a million is. Along with some product we're returning: powder has been stepped on so many times it's baby food.

Nervous now, Yayo is staring at the guy with the wool shirt.

YAYO: You suppose to give me the focking money yourself.

Bo Catlett gets up, adjusts his suit jacket, smoothing the long roll lapel.

BO CATLETT: Try to be cool Yahoo. I told you where it is. Do it how I told you and have a safe trip home. Or as you all say, *vaya con Dios*, motherfucker.

Bo Catlett walks off, leaving Yayo sitting there, confused now, not quite sure what to do.

CLOSE ON HAND HOLDING TICKET ENVELOPE

The name Y. PORTILLO written on the jacket.

PULL BACK TO REVEAL: BAGGAGE CLAIM – DAY

Where the Big Man in the Hawaiian Shirt waits by the carousel. His LITTLE GIRL HOLDS THE TICKET ENVELOPE. The man grabs a case from the carousel and walks to the door. He tears the baggage claim stub from the envelope and hands it to the SECURITY GUARD.

EXT. BAGGAGE CLAIM – DAY

As the Big Man and the little girl walk to the black stretch parked at the curb, RONNIE WINGATE, an aging surfer in a suede jacket and running shoes, holds the door open for them.

RONNIE: Like fucking clockwork, eh Bear?

BEAR/BIG MAN: Don't cuss in front of Farrah.

The Bear hands the case to Bo Catlett who sits in the back of the limo . . .

GIRL: Hi, Bo.

BO CATLETT: How you doing, sweetie?

As Ronnie gets in back with Bo Catlett, The Bears puts his daughter in a toddler seat up front, then gets behind the wheel.

GIRL: Here we go!

EXT. HARRY'S OFFICE – DAY

Two stories, part of a block of white storefronts on Sunset near La Cienega.

INT. HARRY'S OFFICE – DAY

Light filters through venetian blinds, illuminating a desk stacked with folders, magazines, scripts, papers, unopened mail, hotel ashtrays, a brass lamp, a clock and two telephones.

HARRY: I once asked this literary agent what type of writing brought the most money and the agent says, 'Ransom notes.'

Chili stands looking over some of the old photographs as Harry goes through the mess on the desk. There are some of Karen, Harry with a much younger, blonde Karen. Harry with giant bugs, Harry shaking hands with mutants and maniacs, and so on.

HARRY: Here it is . . . Mr. Lovejoy.

Harry hands a script to Chili. Chili examines the cover, the first time he's ever held a movie script. He opens it to the middle . . .

CHILI: *Lovejoy sits behind the wheel, watching the bar across the street, getting his video camera ready for action . . .*

(looks up)

What's he doing? Following a guy?

HARRY: Read it. It's a grabber.

Chili looks out the window as we see a long black stretch limo pull up to the curb down on the street . . .

CHILI: Hey, Harry? I think your investors are here.

EXT. HARRY'S OFFICE – SAME TIME

As the Bear opens the door for Bo Catlett and Ronnie . . .

INT. HARRY'S OFFICE – SAME TIME

As Harry moves away from the window.

HARRY: Jesus . . .

Chili tosses the script on the desk, moves between a pair of fat red leather chairs.

CHILI: All right, Harry, make sure the limo guys sit here, not over on the sofa.

Harry is tugging the string to lower the blinds behind the desk.

CHILI: No leave 'em up, we want the light in their eyes. I'll be at the desk . . . but don't introduce me, let it go, just start talking. You're gonna be here, behind 'em when they sit down.

HARRY: They'll be looking at you. They don't know who you are.

CHILI: That's right, they're wondering, who's this guy? You don't tell 'em. Understand, Harry? *Do not tell 'em who I am.*

Harry glances off as we hear RONNIE SINGING down the hall.

RONNIE: *(O.S.)* In the year 2525 . . . if man is still alive . . .

HARRY: So what do I say to them?

CHILI: You don't say any more'n you have to. You say, 'Well, I'm glad you assholes stopped by, so I can set you straight.'

HARRY: You're kidding, right?

RONNIE: *(O.S.) If woman can sur-vive . . .*

CHILI: You tell 'em the movie's been postponed. Say, till next year, if you want. But don't tell 'em why or what you're doing. Understand, Harry? You don't tell 'em *anything* about *Mr. Lovejoy.*

And the door opens. Chili sits behind the desk, watching the two of them come into the office. Ronnie singing . . .

RONNIE: *They may find . . .*

He looks about the office . . . at the old photographs . . .

RONNIE: Harry, what year is it, man? We enter a time warp? I feel like I'm back in Hollywood of yesteryear.

Harry waves them right into the two cracked red leather chairs facing the desk. Chili watches as Catlett comes first. Sitting down, he nods to Chili who ignores him.

HARRY: Have a seat . . . right over here . . .

Ronnie sits down in the chair and hooks one leg over the arm, swings it up and down, his motor running on some chemical. He too stares at Chili . . .

HARRY: This is my associate, Chili Palmer, who'll be working with me.

Harry already forgetting his instructions. Chili can't believe it. The limo guys nod to Chili and Chili nods back, trying to catch Harry's eye.

HARRY: I want to make sure there's no misunderstanding here. Despite rumors you might have heard, your investment in *Freaks* is as sound as the day you signed your participation agreement.

Ronnie has his face raised to the ceiling.

RONNIE: I can hear you, but where the fuck are you, man?

BO CATLETT: *(looking at Chili)* What I been wondering is where's he been.

RONNIE: Yeah, where've you been? We haven't heard from you lately.

Harry comes around to stand at one side of the desk, his back to the window . . .

HARRY: I've been off scouting locations. Interviewing actors in New York.

Chili's gaze moves from Ronnie the fool to Bo Catlett the dude, the man composed, elbows on the chair arms, his hands steepled in front of him.

HARRY: The main thing I want to tell you, the start date for *Freaks* is being pushed back a little, a few months.

Ronnie stops bouncing his leg.

RONNIE: A few months?

HARRY: Maybe longer. We need prep time.

RONNIE: Hey, Harry? Bullshit. We have an agreement with you, man.

HARRY: We're gonna make the picture. I've just got another project to do first, that's all. One I promised this guy years ago.

Chili shakes his head, he can't believe he's hearing this. Ronnie sits up straight.

RONNIE: I want to see your books, Harry. Show me where it is, a two with five zeroes after it in black and white, man. I want to see your books and your bank statements.

CHILI: Hey, Ronnie? Look at me.

Boom. Ronnie looks over. So does Bo Catlett for that matter.

CHILI: You have a piece of a movie, that's all. You don't have a piece of Harry. He told you we're doing another movie first. And that's the way it's gonna be.

RONNIE: Excuse me. But who the fuck are you?

CHILI: I'm the one telling you how it is. That's not too hard to figure out, is it?

Ronnie turns to Bo Catlett, the man not having moved or changed his expression the last few minutes.

RONNIE: Cat?

Bo Catlett takes his time, gives it some thought. He looks at Harry . . .

BO CATLETT: What's this movie you're doing first?

CHILI: Harry, let me answer that.

Catlett looks at Chili again.

CHILI: But first I want to know who I'm talking to. Am I talking to you, or am I talking to him?

BO CATLETT: *(beat, smiles)* You can talk to me.

CHILI: That's what I thought. So let me put it this way: Outside of *Freaks*, it's not any of your fuckin' business what we do.

Now it's between them. The guy studies Chili, thinks about whether or not to make a move, when Harry steps in, reaches over the desk and picks up a script . . .

HARRY: This is the project, *Mr. Lovejoy*. I'm not trying to pull anything on you guys. This is it, right here.

Chili looks at Harry, wonders if there's a way to shut him up without punching him in the mouth.

RONNIE: *Mr. Loveboy?* What is it, Harry, a porno flick?

He reaches for the script. Harry backs away, holds the script to his chest. Bo Catlett notices this.

HARRY: It's nothing. It's fluff. Nothing you'd be interested in.

Bo Catlett eyes him a beat, then pushes out of his chair . . .

BO CATLETT: Harry, you think we go to see your movies? I've seen better film on teeth. Makes no difference to me which one our money's in. So how 'bout you take our twenty points out of *Freaks* and put 'em in this other one, *Mr. Loverboy*.

HARRY: I can't do it.

BO CATLETT: You positive about that?

HARRY: It's a different kind of deal.

Bo Catlett nods, gets up.

BO CATLETT: Okay. Then be good enough to hand us our money back, or you think about us coming in on this new one.

RONNIE: By Friday, man, or you're fuckin' dead as disco.

Ronnie opens his coat so that Harry can see a gun tucked in his belt . . .

RONNIE: You hear me?

Bo Catlett gives Ronnie a look.

BO CATLETT: Take your time, Harry.

(closes Ronnie's jacket)

We're not animals. Are we, Ronnie?

Bo Catlett glances once more at Chili then follows Ronnie out the door. Harry stares at the door a moment, senses Chili staring at him . . .

HARRY: What?

CHILI: I don't know, maybe I wasn't clear. But I *thought* . . . I told you to keep your mouth shut.

HARRY: I had to tell 'em *something*.

CHILI: Never say *anything* unless you have to.

Chili shakes his head as Harry sits down in one of the chairs, fumbles for his cigarettes.

CHILI: You tell me you want these guys off your back. Next thing I know, you're saying yeah, maybe they can have a piece of *Mr. Lovejoy*. I couldn't believe my fuckin' ears.

HARRY: I said I'd think about it. What does that mean? In this town, nothing.

CHILI: That's the difference between you and me, Harry. I say what I mean. I want something from someone, I ask 'em straight out. I want Martin Weir, I go get Martin Weir. I don't fuck around with his trainer's shrink.

HARRY: His shrink's trainer.

Chili looks at Harry.

CHILI: Take me back to my car.

EXT. LAX – DAY

As a plane touches down on the runway . . .

INT. SOVEREIGN TERMINAL – SAME TIME

Yayo, now soaked with sweat, is still here. He stands watching a row of lockers. He stares at one of them . . .

CLOSE ON LOCKER.

The number C-18. We PUSH IN . . .

YAYO

starts to move for it . . . then looks off at . . .

A MAN IN A SUIT

*as we quickly TILT DOWN to the guy's ankle, looks
like a bulge there. We then . . .*

WHIP PAN TO

*A WOMAN, dressed casually in slacks and a blouse. We
TILT DOWN to her ankle, hmmm, is that a bulge?
We . . .*

WHIP PAN TO

*A TENNIS SHOE, tapping to some unheard rhythm
and what looks like a bulge near the ankle. We TILT UP
this time to reveal A LITTLE KID, listening to a
walkman.*

YAYO

*obviously losing it now, rubs his eyes and quickly walks off
to a row of payphones . . .*

EXT. KAREN FLORES' HOUSE – DAY

Chili's minivan is parked out front.

TOMMY: *(V.O.)* Where you been? I been callin'
all over for you . . .

INT. KAREN'S HOUSE – THE STUDY – SAME

TIME

Chili sits at the desk on the phone.

TOMMY: *(PHONE)* Ray Bones is looking for you. He's got some kinda bug up his ass, can't sit still.

INT. BARBER SHOP – DAY

Tommy on the phone.

TOMMY: I hate to say I told you, but I did. I told you don't start nothing with him that time.

INTERCUTTING TOMMY & CHILI:

CHILI: You said don't say nothing and I didn't.

TOMMY: No, you just broke his fuckin' nose instead.

CHILI: You gonna start that again? You're just like him, all you got room for in your brain is one fuckin' thing.

TOMMY: All I know is he came by the barber shop, all fuckin' undone, wanting to know where you were staying in Vegas. I told him I don't know. I still don't.

CHILI: How'd he know I was in Vegas? You tell him?

TOMMY: He already knew it.

CHILI: Yeah, well, I'm in L. A. now.

TOMMY: Whatta you doing out there?

CHILI: I'm going into the movie business.

TOMMY: What're you talking about? You wanna be a movie star?

CHILI: I'm thinking about producing.

TOMMY: How you gonna do that? You don't know shit about making movies.

CHILI: I don't think the producer has to do much, outside of maybe knowing a writer.

TOMMY: Hey, Chil? I think you're fulla shit.

INT. KAREN'S ENTRY WAY – SAME TIME

As Karen, dressed as a B-movie queen, press kit under one arm steps inside, freezes as she hears . . .

CHILI: *(O.S.)* . . . call me soon as you know when Ray's coming out.

INT. STUDY – SAME TIME

Chili is scribbling something on a piece of paper as Karen comes into the room. Chili looks up at her as he hangs up, smiles at her.

CHILI: Hey . . . Karen. How ya' doin'?

KAREN: What're you doing here?

CHILI: I wanted to come by, apologize for coming into your house like I did last night.

KAREN: Lemme get this straight, you broke in *again* to apologize for breaking in before?

CHILI: No, no . . . you left the patio door open. You gotta stop doin' that, all the nice things you got around here.

KAREN: Yeah, well make sure you lock it on the way out.

CHILI: Rough day on the set?

KAREN: I spent all day crawling out of a grave. The costumer kept bitching 'cause I was ripping my nylons –

CHILI: Ripped nylons work. Makes the shot more real.

KAREN: *(regarding him)* . . . That's what we finally decided.

CHILI: Like in *Bride of the Mutant*, when you played the whole end with that torn top.

She looks at him.

KAREN: You saw that one?

CHILI: Yeah. When you turn to the camera to tell the alien mother that her time on earth is finished . . . when you give us all that look, Joan Crawford wishes on her best day she had that much presence. Not even in *Mildred Pierce* – which by the way was a better book than a movie – did Crawford even touch the intensity you had in that look.

KAREN: *(beat)* Yeah . . . that was a good scene. I mean, for a horror movie.

CHILI: For *any* movie.

KAREN: I know I'm better than what I've been doing the last ten years, walking around in a tank top and fuck-me pumps, waiting till it's time to scream.

CHILI: Man, can you scream.

KAREN: Yeah. It's a real gift.

(beat)

I'm just saying it'd be nice, one time in my career to get the chance to say one great line. You know, like in that Bette Davis picture, *Cabin in the . . .*

CHILI: *Cotton.*

KAREN: Yeah, you know when Bette comes up to the guy on the porch, gives him a flirty look and says, 'I'd kiss you, but . . .'

CHILI/KAREN: 'I just washed my hair.'

KAREN: Yeah.

CHILI: That is a great line.

Chili looks at her . . .

CHILI: How come you stopped making movies with Harry?

KAREN: I married Martin. That was a full-time job.

CHILI: You read Harry's new one? He says it's the best thing he's ever read.

KAREN: He must mean after *Slime Creature 3*.

CHILI: That why Harry came over last night? See if you could help him get Martin in his movie?

KAREN: Harry's dreaming of a forty-million-dollar production he'll never get off the ground with a star he'll never sign. With or without my help.

CHILI: Harry told me Martin loves it, he flipped.

KAREN: Yeah, well Martin is known for his flipping. He flips over a script, and when the time comes to make a deal, he flips out.

CHILI: Tell you what, I'll stop by Harry's office and pick up a copy for you.

KAREN: Don't go out of your way.

They consider each other a moment . . . until Chili finally checks his watch.

CHILI: Well, I gotta have a talk with Leo, my runaway dry cleaner.

KAREN: Right. See how your story ends.

CHILI: Yeah. Right.

(then)

Listen, *Touch of Evil*'s playing near my hotel. You wanna go check it out? Watch Charlton Heston play a Mexican?

Karen looks caught, doesn't answer right away.

CHILI: Maybe some other time.

He turns to go, then turns back to her . . .

CHILI: 'He tried to make love to me and I shot him.'

(then)

Another great Bette Davis line.

Karen looks at him. Surprised. He smiles at her.

CHILI: See you around.

EXT. BEVERLY HILLS HOTEL – NIGHT

Leo Devoe, dressed in a sporty plaid ensemble, complete with little matching hat gets out of a cab, and walks to the front entrance. He tips the doorman, gives him a grin.

DOORMAN: Evening, sir.

LEO: And a good evening to you, too, sir.

INT. HOTEL HALLWAY – NIGHT

As Leo the high-rolling dry cleaner bounces down the hall, unlocks his door . . .

INT. LEO'S HOTEL ROOM – NIGHT

Dark. Leo enters, heads for the bottle of Chivas on the desk. Has one straight out of the bottle, ahhh, before pulling a fat wad of cash out of his jacket, tossing it on the desk like it's change from the cab fare.

He then takes off the jacket, unbuttons the shirt, reaches for the Chivas again, when we hear . . .

CHILI: *(O.S.)* Look at me, Leo.

Crash. Something glass hits the floor. Probably the Chivas bottle as Leo nearly has a fucking coronary . . .

Leo looks over as Chili turns on the light behind him. But what catches Leo's eye is the BRIEFCASE sitting on the couch beside Chili.

CHILI: I wouldn't think you're that dumb, leave over three hundred grand in the closet, underneath the extra blanket, but I guess you are.

LEO: I didn't know where else to keep it.

(then)

Where would you?

CHILI: You're here a while, what's wrong with a bank?

LEO: They report it to the IRS.

CHILI: You don't open an account, Leo, you put it in a safe deposit box. Dip in whenever you want.

Leo nods in his sporty hat and undershirt, thinking it over, what to do the next time he scams an airline.

CHILI: You've been losing.

LEO: I'm up twelve grand today.

CHILI: From when? You left Vegas with four-fifty?

LEO: Who told you that?

CHILI: Now you're down to three-ten in the case. You must've cooled off quite a bit since you got here.

LEO: How'd you know I was here?

CHILI: Here's another tip: next time you write a note to your wife, don't use hotel stationery.

Leo looks away, raises his preshaped plaid hat and recocks it, then . . .

LEO: It was Fay, wasn't it, told you about the money. She tell you my whole life history, for Christ's sake?

CHILI: I wouldn't let her if she tried. Why I'm here, Leo, basically, is to save your ass.

LEO: How? By taking my money?

CHILI: You can keep what you won today. That's yours.

LEO: It's all mine.

CHILI: Sit down, Leo.

Leo sits down in the arm chair, stares sadly at the briefcase.

CHILI: I don't know how you got this far, you're so fuckin' dumb. But now you're through. I'm gonna explain to you why and I hope you're not too dumb to understand what I'm saying. Okay?

Leo nods.

CHILI: Ray Bones is now the man you're dealing with. Ray Bones finds out what you did, he's gonna want everything you have. And when I say everything, I mean even that sporty little hat if he wants it. Then after he takes all you got, he'll most likely hit you with some kind of heavy object if he doesn't shoot you, just so you won't tell on him.

Chili lets that sink in a minute.

CHILI: I won't do that. Take your stuff or hurt you. You have three-ten in the case, right? I'm gonna take the three hundred you scammed off the airline, but the rest of it, the ten grand? I'm gonna borrow that and pay you back sometime.

Leo's squinting at him now . . .

LEO: You take all my money, but you're borrowing part of it?

CHILI: At eighteen percent, okay? And don't ask me no more fuckin' questions. I'm leaving.

He picks up the briefcase as he rises from the sofa and Leo gets out of his chair.

LEO: But you won't know where I am. I don't even know where I'll be.

CHILI: I'll find you, Leo . . .

Chili reaches for the door, opens it and looks back at Leo . . .

CHILI: You leave a trail like a fuckin' caterpillar.

INT. HALLWAY – SAME TIME

As Chili starts for the elevator. Leo steps into his doorway . . .

LEO: Wait a minute. What's this eighteen-percent-a-year shit? You want to borrow ten, the vig's three bills a week. Fifteen for the vig plus the ten, that's twenty-five big ones you go a whole year, buddy! You hear me?

Chili stops, turns around. As he starts back, he sees Leo's scared look just before he slams the door shut. Chili shakes his head, starts back for the elevator.

EXT. GRIFFITH PARK – NIGHT

Chili drives a dark road up into the park. He rounds a corner, and we see an explosion of light up ahead as we come upon . . .

A MOVIE SET

Chili pulls in behind a row of trailers. He gets out of the car and heads for the set where Harry is now looking up at the sky and yelling at someone . . .

HARRY: How's anyone gonna see anything from way up there?

CHILI: Hey, Harry.

HARRY: Yeah, Chili. Hi.

(looking up)

You're fifty feet in the air!

The DIRECTOR – early twenties, dressed like a frat boy – sits on a crane about fifty feet above the set . . .

DIRECTOR: Harry. I'm gonna boom down real fast, get a subjective p-o-v.

CHILI: Listen, I talked to Karen. She's gonna think about helping you out.

HARRY: Yeah, but *whose* point of view?

DIRECTOR: Whatta you mean, whose point of view? The *audience's* point of view.

HARRY: Get down here. I wanna talk to you. Come on . . . right now . . .

(to Chili)

She's gonna talk to Martin?

CHILI: She's thinking about it. I just need the key to your office. I just told her I'd pick up a script.

Harry tosses Chili a key-ring.

HARRY: It's the red one. Take it off the ring.

Chili sits down in one of the director's chairs that sits off to one side. He starts to take the key off the ring . . .

VOICE: Your name Vicky Vespa?

Chili looks up at a bored-looking ACTRESS standing there in a blood-soaked nightie.

CHILI: Excuse me?

ACTRESS: I asked you, is your name Vicky Vespa?

CHILI: No.

ACTRESS: Then get the fuck outta my chair.

Chili sits forward, sees her name printed on the back. He

gets up. As she sits down, we see an ICE PICK sticking out the other side of her head. Chili sits back down next to her in the chair with HARRY ZIMM on the back.

HARRY: *(to the director)* What're you doing? I thought I told you to get down here?

The kid nods to the camera operator who lowers the crane as we BOOM WAY UP . . .

HARRY: All these camera moves and weird angles and shit are gonna distance us from the emotion of the scene.

DIRECTOR: What 'emotion?' Girl just got stabbed in the ear with an ice pick.

HARRY: She's scared! Fear is an emotion!

(then)

Look, kid, if you remember anything from your time working with Harry Zimm, let it be the three key words to filmmaking.

The kid fiddles with the crane controls.

DIRECTOR: Yeah? What three words, Harry?

HARRY: Pick 'n' Save.

DIRECTOR: Hm?

HARRY: You heard me, Pick 'n' Save.

Harry turns so the rest of the crew can hear him . . .

HARRY: Now I'm gonna tell you a little story, happened to me years ago when I was so broke I had to go to the Pick 'n' Save over on Vine to buy a lousy candybar for my dinner.

Chili watches the crew stop what they're doing and listen.

HARRY: I'm standing in line waiting to pay my two bits when I overhear this lady, call her Mildred, talking to the cashier about a movie.

The Director gives a look to his assistant like 'Jesus, you believe this shit?'

HARRY: So Mildred says to the cashier, 'I saw the new Streisand picture.'

(gets into it the way Mildred did)

'God, I just love it at the end when she brushed Robert Redford's hair off his forehead the way she did when they were together, and the way they gave each other this look that said they still loved each other, but knew they couldn't be together. That look was so . . . romantic.'

DIRECTOR: That's great, Harry. So what's the –

HARRY: What she did *not* say was, 'I just loved the way the director moved the camera so much it made me fuckin' seasick.' All she cared about was that *look*. All she *remembered* was that look. And why do we remember things in movies? Because *we can see them.*

Harry's right in the guy's face now . . .

HARRY: So . . . *keep this fuckin' camera down here on the ground and shoot this scene, so we can see what the*

*fuck is goin' on, before I get someone over sixteen to
fuckin' shoot it for you!*

*Harry walks over to Chili, sees Chili sitting there. Chili
tosses Harry his key ring.*

CHILI: Here's your keys, Harry.

HARRY: Get the fuck outta my chair.

EXT. HARRY ZIMM'S OFFICE – NIGHT

*As Chili pulls out front, gets out of the minivan, he looks
up, sees a light on in Harry's office.*

INT. CORRIDOR – NIGHT

*Chili walks down the hallway, dark except for a light on
at the end of the hall . . .*

INT. HARRY'S OFFICE – NIGHT

*Bo Catlett, reading glasses, script open in front of him,
looks up from Harry's desk as Chili steps into the office.*

BO CATLETT: This ain't bad, you know it? This
Mr. Lovejoy. Needs a better ending but yeah, I can
see why Harry wants to do it.

*Chili says nothing, sits down in one of the red leather
chairs.*

BO CATLETT: You understand I knew Harry
was lying, saying this wasn't any good, but holding
on to it, man, like you have to break his fingers to
get it from him.

CHILI: That's funny, I was just wondering what I

was gonna break of yours to get it away from *you.*

Bo Catlett smiles at him, doesn't give up the script.

BO CATLETT: I'm just explaining to you what I'm doing here. Case you think I come to rob the place, rip off any of this dusty old shit the man has.

CHILI: I'd never make you as a burglar, not in that outfit.

Bo Catlett sits back in the chair a moment, watches Chili light a cigarette . . .

BO CATLETT: Harry called you his associate, but what does that mean? I never heard your name or read it in *Variety* or *The Reporter* or anyplace.

CHILI: It's what he said, I'm his associate.

BO CATLETT: You must bring something heavy to the deal.

CHILI: That's right, me.

Bo Catlett picks up a piece of paper off the desk . . .

BO CATLETT: Says here you're getting Martin Weir for the part of Lovejoy.

CHILI: Yeah, we're getting Martin.

BO CATLETT: No shit, come on. How you gonna do that?

CHILI: I put a gun right here . . .

(touches the side of his head)

. . . and I tell him, 'Sign the paper Marty or your fuckin' dead.' Like that.

BO CATLETT: I wonder, would that work?

(then)

You know who I see for Al Roxy? Harvey Keitel. The man could do it in his sleep.

CHILI: Harvey Keitel. Yeah. Maybe. He was pretty good in the movie *Fingers*.

BO CATLETT: I missed that one. Or, hey, you know who else? Morgan Freeman. You know Morgan?

CHILI: Yeah, Morgan Freeman. But he's a colored guy.

BO CATLETT: So what? Where's it say in this script he's white? Color is what the part needs, man, somebody to do it has some style. The way it is now, Ronnie could do it, play himself, some cracked out asshole.

(then)

So whatta you think of the script?

Bo watches as Chili picks up a copy of the script, begins flipping through it.

CHILI: Title's the first thing's got to go. And the guy's name. I mean, even this writer's name, Murray Saffrin is better than Lovejoy.

BO CATLETT: I'm with you on that. And don't

you think it needs a good female part? Increase the romance angle.

Chili flips through the script, sees a name . . .

CHILI: There's Ilona.

BO CATLETT: What about her?

CHILI: Get something going there.

BO CATLETT: With Ilona? You know how old Ilona is?

CHILI: She's . . . young.

BO CATLETT: Young? She's fuckin' nine-years-old, same age as Lovejoy's kid. Bernie. One she calls Bernard. Have you read the script?

CHILI: Yeah, I read it. I was just thinking you could make her older. We might even be able to get Karen Flores.

BO CATLETT: Who?

CHILI: She's been out of movies a few years, but she's good. Real good.

Bo Catlett studies Chili a moment, smiles . . .

BO CATLETT: You know what I'm thinkin'?

(leans forward)

You wanna make the girl older. I don't like the ending. We could do that, you and me, sit down and write the script over where it needs it.

Chili flips through the script a moment . . .

CHILI: You know how to write one of these?

BO CATLETT: There's nothin' to know? You have an idea, you write down what you wanna say. Then you get somebody to add in the commas and shit where they belong, if you aren't positive yourself. Maybe fix up the spelling where you have some tricky words . . . although I've seen scripts where I *know* words weren't spelled right and there was hardly any commas in it at all. So I don't think it's too important. Anyway, you come to the last page you write in 'Fade out' and that's the end, you're done.

CHILI: That's all there is to it, huh?

BO CATLETT: That's all.

Chili sits forward, stubs out his cigarette, exhales into Bo Catlett's face . . .

CHILI: Then what do I need *you* for?

Bo Catlett starts for the door.

BO CATLETT: I really think I can be of service on this one.

CHILI: Yeah, well, we need a ride somewhere, we'll let you know.

EXT. NUART THEATER – NIGHT

As Karen walks up to the box office. A Touch of Evil *on the marquis.*

INT. MOVIE THEATER – NIGHT

Not so full. Chili sits in the middle, watching the final scene as Orson Welles gets blown away, falls into the oily river. He can't take his eyes off the screen . . .

Karen comes in, starts up the aisle, looking for Chili. She spots him, just as he mouths the dialogue along with Marlene Dietrich . . .

MARLENE DIETRICH: *(O.S.)* He was some kind of man.

Karen smiles, decides to wait a moment. Chili, lost in the movie . . . keeps mouthing the dialogue . . .

MARLENE DIETRICH: *(O.S.)* What does it matter what you say about people?

MORT MILLS: *(O.S.)* Good-bye, Tanya.

MARLENE DIETRICH: *Adios.*

As Tanya/Marlene Dietrich resumes her slow walk away, Karen sits down at the end of the row. People start getting up to leave. Chili turns to a GUY a few seats away from him . . .

CHILI: Wow, huh?

The guy gives Chili a look, puts his arm around his DATE, and quickly starts up the aisle so that Chili can now see Karen sitting there at the end of the row . . .

CHILI: You been here the whole time?

KAREN: I just caught the end.

She gets up, they start up the aisle together . . .

CHILI: You know, Welles didn't even wanna do that one. Some studio made him do it. He owed 'em one and all his own movies lost money.

(walking out now)

But, hey, sometimes that's when you do your best work, you got a gun to your head . . .

EXT. NUART – NIGHT

As Karen and Chili exit the theater, stand there a moment.

CHILI: I got you a copy of the script.

KAREN: I already read it. Harry left a copy at the house.

CHILI: What do you think?

She starts walking . . .

KAREN: I think it's not horrible.

CHILI: I don't like the title. Or the main guy's name.

KAREN: Then you've read it?

CHILI: Not yet.

KAREN: You and Harry'll make a great team.

(then)

I'm gonna make a deal with him.

CHILI: There a part in it for you?

KAREN: I don't want to act in it, I want to *produce* it with Harry. Especially if I help him get Martin.

CHILI: Sounds fair.

KAREN: What do you get out of it?

He stops, looks at her.

CHILI: That why you came over here, to ask me that?

KAREN: I want to know.

CHILI: Why does anyone want to be in movies?

KAREN: Yesterday, you were a loan shark.

He starts walking again . . .

CHILI: I was never much into it. All that bullshit having to do with respect. It's bad enough having to treat those guys like they're your heroes, having to smile when they make some stupid remark they think's real funny.

KAREN: And you think the movie business is any different?

CHILI: Yeah well . . . I like movies. I figure if I help Harry make one, I'll find out what you have to do outside of have an idea and raise the money. That doesn't sound too hard. I was in the money business and I get ideas all the time.

They stop at her car.

KAREN: I'm talking to Martin tomorrow morning. I told Harry I'd meet you and him at Abiquiu afterward.

(opens her door)

This might work, you never know.

He stands there, watching her drive away.

EXT. HARRY'S APARTMENT BUILDING – NIGHT

Just above Franklin in the Hollywood Hills. A realtor might call it Chandleresque. We call it old and cheap.

INT. HARRY'S APARTMENT – NIGHT

Continuing on the old and cheap theme. Harry stands behind the wet bar pouring himself a strong one. He looks at himself in the smoke-tinted mirror squares, downs the drink in one and pours himself another.

A KNOCK AT THE DOOR.

Harry looks at the door.

HARRY: Who is it?

WOMAN'S VOICE: Me.

HARRY: *(lower)* Fuck.

WOMAN'S VOICE: I heard that.

Harry moves to the door and opens it to reveal DORIS SAFFRIN – fiftyish, fur coat, hair up so that we can see the nifty necklace. She leans in the doorway . . .

HARRY: Hello, Doris.

DORIS: Harry Zimm. You look like a wet kiss.

And she plants one on him. Walks into the apartment. Looking good for her age. Hell, for any age.

DORIS: Well, aren't you gonna offer me whatever it is you taste like?

HARRY: Come on in.

Doris goes to the window. Harry goes to the bar, pours them each a drink . . .

DORIS: What a spectacular view.

HARRY: Yeah, lovely. Last night I watched two guys carjack a Camero down on the corner of Argyle there.

(hands her the drink)

What do you want, Doris?

She drinks, never taking her eyes off him.

DORIS: I miss Murray, Harry.

HARRY: Yeah, me too. He was a helluva good writer. And I would know. I discovered him. Made him what he was.

DORIS: What he was, was a hack, couldn't get a job writing for anybody but you.

(off Harry)

I'm being honest. He was a lousy writer, but he was

a good husband. I just didn't know it until too late.

Harry finishes his drink, pours himself another . . .

HARRY: Yeah, well, twenty–twenty hindsight and all that.

Harry takes a big, noisy pull off his drink as she moves to the bar . . .

DORIS: I hate being alone. The house is so quiet. So lonely. It needs . . .

(studies him)

A man's touch.

And with that, she opens up the fur coat to reveal that she's wearing nothing but a garter belt and high heels.

HARRY: Nice garter.

She sets her drink down, moves in, wraps her arms around his neck . . .

HARRY: I'm not sure how I feel about this, Doris.

DORIS: *(reaching down)* You seem to feel fine about it.

HARRY: I mean morally. Murray was my friend.

DORIS: Murray's dead.

She kisses him . . . Harry pulls back . . .

HARRY: So this means you've reconsidered our deal on *Mr. Lovejoy*?

DORIS: No. But now that you mention it, I *did*

talk to a handsome executive at Paramount the other day . . . who just happened to get his hands on the script.

HARRY: Yeah, what'd he have to say?

DORIS: He said if Martin's interested, I could get a half a million for it easy. But don't worry, Harry, I'm still giving you until Friday.

HARRY: How honorable of you.

Now she backs away, gives him a hurt look.

DORIS: Harry. If you want me to go, just say the word.

Harry looks at her a moment, decides . . .

HARRY: What the hell . . .

. . . And pulls her as close as we then . . .

DISSOLVE TO:

EXT. HOLLYWOOD HILLS HOME – NIGHT

We hear laughter, rock and roll as a NUDE WOMAN dives into a blue-lit swimming pool and swims the length . . .

We then TILT UP to a HOUSE ON STILTS above this one and see the lone figure of Bo Catlett standing on his deck.

EXT. BO CATLETT'S HOUSE – NIGHT

The shimmering yellow grid of the city in the b.g., Bo Catlett, barefoot, bathrobe, leans on the rail of his deck, watching the folks frolic twelve stories down.

YAYO: *(V.O.)* Listen to me, man, I don't wan' no focking key. I wan' the *money*.

EXT. BO CATLETT'S DECK – NIGHT

Bo Catlett looks inside where Yayo paces back and forth. The Bear reclines on a chaise lounge.

BO CATLETT: Hey, Yayo? You gonna smoke, get the hell off my seventy-bucks-a-yard carpet.

Yayo steps out on to the deck . . .

BO CATLETT: I told you where the money is. All you gotta do is go get it.

YAYO: No. I'll tell *you* something: I go to the airport and they bus' me, I tell them I was getting something for *you*, tha's all I know.

BO CATLETT: Tha's all you know, huh? Wait here a minute, Yayo, I be back directly.

Yayo leans against the railing, cuts a 'now that's the way you get things done' look at the Bear. He lights a cigarette, looks o.s. and freezes . . .

YAYO: The fock you doing with that?

Bo Catlett holds a big .45 out in front of him . . .

BO CATLETT: I'm taking you out, Yahoo.

. . . and shoots Yayo in the chest, the gun going off loud, the round knocking the little Latin man back against the railing.

BO CATLETT: Dead focking center, man.

Yayo, a stupid look on his face, stumbles backwards, over the railing. The Bear reaches for him, but it's too late . . .

EXT. HOUSE DOWN BELOW – SAME TIME

The group down here is too stoned to notice the little Colombian who falls from the deck high above like a sack of dirt, then slides partway down the slope.

EXT. BO CATLETT'S DECK – SAME TIME

The bear looks over at Bo Catlett . . . who now calmly stares down at the motionless form of Yayo.

BO CATLETT: Shit, now someone's gotta climb down there and get him.

BEAR: You didn't have to shoot him, Bo. We coulda just beat him up some.

BO CATLETT: You see that? The way the man just went right over?

Bo Catlett takes a sip of his drink, looks at the railing.

BO CATLETT: Maybe we can get Chili Palmer up here. You fix my railing to give way like they do in the movies. Then I invite the man out here, have a look at my view. Get him to lean over the railing, see all the naked people down there . . . a tragic accident, officer . . .

Bear looks at him.

BEAR: Cat, that's the lamest idea I've ever heard.

BO CATLETT: Yeah, well, I'm bored, Bear. I wanna make movies.

Bear looks at him.

BO CATLETT: I mean, what's the point of living in L.A. if you're not in the movie business?

Bo Catlett leans on the railing, looks down at Yayo again.

BO CATLETT: And I mean high up in it.

(turns to Bear)

That's why Harry's gonna make *Mr. Lovejoy* with me, not Chili Palmer.

BEAR: *Mr. Lovejoy?* That's cute, Bo.

BO CATLETT: Doesn't matter what it's called, Harry's got Martin Weir and it's gonna be big.

BEAR: They all sound big at the talking stage.

EXT. MARTIN WEIR'S HOUSE – MORNING

Karen pulls into the driveway in a convertible BMW. As she checks her make-up in the REARVIEW MIRROR, we see Chili pull up behind her in his rented minivan. She turns around, frowns, and quickly gets out of her car.

He gets out of the van . . . holds up a Star Map . . .

CHILI: This thing's actually accurate. I bought it for ten bucks from a kid in a lawn chair on Sunset . . .

KAREN: You were supposed to wait for me with Harry at the restaurant.

Chili points to a star on the map . . .

CHILI: See, here it is . . . Martin Weir's house . . . right across the street from George Hamilton.

VOICE: Chili, Jesús!

They both look to the front door where a tall, skinny WOMAN with wild, jet black hair stands.

WOMAN: It *is* you . . .

She comes bounding down the steps, runs over and gives him a hug . . . Karen can't believe what she sees.

CHILI: Nicole?

WOMAN: It's Nicki now. I don't believe this . . .

CHILI: Me neither.

(to Karen)

We know each other.

Karen smiles: 'How 'bout that.' Then looks at Nicki.

KAREN: Hello, Nicki.

NICKI: Karen. Shit. I didn't see you there. How are you?

Karen starts to answer, but Nicki's already hustling Chili inside . . .

INT. MARTIN WEIR'S HOUSE – DAY

White everything. Way off in the b.g., a view on to the huge backyard. A pool man cleans the pool. A gardener blows the leaves.

Martin's extensive photography collection lines the walls. Chili steps inside, checks some of them out: most of the photographs are of Martin.

NICKI: Martin will be out in a minute.

(to Karen)

Chili was the only one at Momo's didn't hit on me.

KAREN: What a gentleman.

NICKI: You like my hair?

(reaches up, touches it)

Black like this?

CHILI: It's nice. Especially under your arms.

Somehow this makes Karen feel better.

NICKI: Martin won't let me shave. I guess I fill some need. Brings him back to the sixties or something.

Karen turns as we hear a TOILET FLUSH somewhere o.s.

NICKI: *(looks o.s.)* Speak of the devil . . .

Chili follows her gaze and we see . . .

MARTIN

as he comes down the stairs, checking the front of his trousers. He and Karen spot each other. Both look uncomfortable for a fraction of a second, then Martin hurries over to her . . .

MARTIN: Karen. Wow. Look at you . . .

KAREN: Hello, Martin.

He hugs her and hangs on, leaving Nicki and Chili standing there like idiots.

MARTIN: Mmmmm. You smell terrific.

(to Nicki)

She always smelled so good.

NICKI: *(thrilled))* Neat.

(then)

Martin, this is Chili Palmer.

MARTIN: Chili is it?

CHILI: Yeah, a pleasure, Martin.

NICKI: Chili's a gangster. Ran a club I used to play at for another gangster back in Miami. How is Momo these days anyway?

CHILI: Dead.

Karen fights a smile. Nicki nods solemnly . . .

NICKI: Bummer.

(then)

Well, I'll let you all get to your movie talk. Chili, make sure you say good-bye before you leave.

CUT TO: A PORTRAIT OF MARTIN WEIR

Done in cracked oils, the whole bit.

PULL BACK TO REVEAL: MARTIN'S LIVING ROOM

Martin, Karen and Chili all sit on white couches. Martin is checking out Karen, nodding . . .

MARTIN: I'm sitting here, I'm looking at you and I'm having these flashes. You know, flashbacks, of memories.

(touches her hair)

Of *us.*

KAREN: Really.

MARTIN: Yeah and I'm wondering, how did it go wrong? How did it all . . . slip away?

KAREN: 'It' didn't slip away, Martin, *you* did . . . when you went off to fuck Nicki in the middle of my birthday party.

Martin brings his hand back, nods, lost in thought . . .

MARTIN: Yeah. That was a good party.

CHILI: You know, Marty, you were good in *The Cyclone.*

MARTIN: Martin. It was a beautiful role. All I had to do was find the character's center, the stem I'd used to wind him up and he'd play, man, he'd play.

Karen looks like she wants to throw up.

CHILI: Well, you had it down cold. Watching you in the movie, if I didn't know better I'd have to believe you were a made guy and not acting. Even the fink part. I never met a fink and I hope to God I never do, but how you did it must be the way finks act.

MARTIN: A few weeks before shooting, I went back to Bensonhurst, just to listen to you guys. See, I'm Italian, but I grew up in Tarzana. So I wanted to pick up your rhythms of speech.

CHILI: We talk different?

MARTIN: It's more like your attitude. Your tone, your speech patterns demonstrate a certain confidence in yourselves, in your opinions, your indifference to conventional views.

CHILI: You mean like we don't give a shit.

MARTIN: Yeah. Kinda. Anyway, once I have the authentic sounds of speech, the rhythms, man, the patois, I can actually begin to think the way those guys do, get inside their heads.

Chili exchanges a look with Karen who sits back now. Ready to give up.

CHILI: Okay, I'm one of those guys you mentioned. I'm actually one of 'em. What am I thinking?

Martin looks at Chili . . .

MARTIN: Don't get me wrong, I'm not saying an actual metamorphosis takes place. That wouldn't be acting.

Karen looks at Martin, shakes her head.

CHILI: So you don't know what I'm thinking.

MARTIN: No, I don't. Though I have to say I'm curious.

CHILI: So you want to know.

MARTIN: If you'd like to tell me, yeah.

CHILI: I'm thinking of a movie.

MARTIN: One of mine?

CHILI: One we're producing.

MARTIN: With what? Wiseguy money?

Martin cracks himself up. Karen and Chili crack up with him, Karen leaning into Chili . . .

KAREN: Maybe this was a bad idea.

But Chili keeps looking at Martin.

CHILI: Martin, I'm not connected to those people anymore. Not since I walked out of a loan-shark operation in Miami.

MARTIN: What happened? The pressure got to you?

CHILI: Pressure? I'm the one applied the pressure.

Chili sits back. Karen is starting to enjoy Chili's handling of Martin . . .

CHILI: You're an actor, you like to pretend. Imagine you're the shylock. A guy owes you fifteen grand and he skips, leaves town. What do you do?

Chili watches as the movie star hunches over, narrows his shoulders. For a few moments he holds his hands together in front of him, getting a shifty look in his eyes. Karen shakes her head . . .

KAREN: Oh, for Christ's sake –

MARTIN: I know. I'm doing Shylock instead of a shylock. Okay, what's my motivation? The acquisition of money. To collect. Inflict pain if I have to.

Karen watches as Martin stares at Chili, his expression gradually becoming deadpan, sleepy . . .

MARTIN: Guy owes me fifteen large and takes off, I go after him. The fuck you think I do?

CHILI: Martin, look at me.

MARTIN: I'm looking at you.

So is Karen, for that matter.

CHILI: No, I want you to look at me the way I'm looking at you. Put it in your eyes, 'You're mine, asshole,' without saying it.

MARTIN: Like this?

CHILI: What you're telling me, you're tired? You wanna go to bed?

MARTIN: Wait. How about this?

CHILI: Now you're squinting like you need glasses.

Karen looks away now, fighting a smile.

CHILI: *Look at me.* I'm thinking, You're mine. I fuckin' own you. What I'm *not* doing is feeling anything about it one way or the other. You understand? You're not a person to me, you're a name in my collection book, a guy owes me money, that's all.

Martin nods, gives Chili a nice dead-eyed look. Karen is thoroughly enjoying Chili's manipulation of Martin.

MARTIN: How about this?

CHILI: That's not bad.

MARTIN: That's what I think of you, asshole. Nothing.

CHILI: I believe it.

MARTIN: I turn it on when I confront the guy.

CHILI: Yeah, but you haven't found him yet.

(then)

The guy took off for Las Vegas.

MARTIN: How do I know that?

Karen looks at Chili as he sits back . . .

CHILI: The guy's wife tells you . . .

INT. ABIQUIU RESTAURANT – DAY

Two floors, the upstairs with a railing overlooking the bar. Harry, a drink in front of him, sits in a big corner booth upstairs. He checks his watch . . .

VOICE: Harry, how you doing?

Harry looks up to see Bo Catlett, dressed up as usual, standing there with the Bear, wearing a Hawaiian shirt.

HARRY: Bo. I'm great. Listen, I'm expecting some people –

BO CATLETT: You must be makin' some big deals, doin' lunch in a place like this?

HARRY: I'm working on a few things.

BO CATLETT: Yeah, I hear you bagged Martin Weir for *Mr. Lovejoy.*

HARRY: Boy, this town. Word gets around, doesn't it?

Harry chuckles, takes a sip of his drink.

BO CATLETT: Chili Palmer told me.

Harry's smile goes away.

BO CATLETT: Last night. When he called me over to your office to talk about it.

HARRY: Chili Palmer showed you my script?

BO CATLETT: Yeah, I was wondering why he should do that.

INT. MARTIN WEIR'S HOUSE – SAME TIME

Martin is leaning forward . . . Hooked . . .

MARTIN: The wife sues the airline.

(nods)

This is a gutsy babe.

CHILI: Good-looking, too.

(turns to look at her)

Like Karen.

Chili smiles at her. Martin leans forward.

MARTIN: So when do I meet up with the husband and give him the look?

CHILI: It's not that simple. You have to be careful. There's another guy that comes along, a hard-on you owe some money to. A mob guy. Wants to take you out anyway, on account of a past situation.

MARTIN: Okay. I'm listening.

Chili stops; he doesn't know what else to say. Martin waits, then looks at him a moment . . .

CHILI: At that point, basically, that has to be it.

MARTIN: You're not going to tell me the rest?

KAREN: Well actually, Martin the movie we came to talk about is *Mr. Lovejoy*.

CHILI: Yeah. We understand you read the script and like it . . . a lot.

MARTIN: Refresh my memory . . .

CONTINUED: INT. ABIQUIU – SAME TIME

Harry drains his drink. Bo Catlett exchanges a look with

the Bear, then . . .

BO CATLETT: Listen, Harry, how would you like to get your hands on five hundred grand? You pay me back at your convenience, no interest.

HARRY: You serious?

BO CATLETT: All I want in return is to work on the movie with you. Fact I already got some ideas on how to fix it up.

Bo Catlett signals the waiter . . .

BO CATLETT: How 'bout another one for Mr. Zimm. A double.

HARRY: You're gonna just give me five hundred grand?

BO CATLETT: We'll talk about that, Harry. But first I gotta know, how'd you hook up with Chili Palmer.

EXT. MARTIN WEIR'S HOUSE – DAY

Karen, Martin, and Chili walk out to the driveway.

MARTIN: Lemme talk to Buddy, set up a meeting.

CHILI: Buddy?

KAREN: Lufkin. His . . . agent.

MARTIN: Yeah, Karen knows him.

KAREN: But you are interested?

MARTIN: I'm intrigued, yeah. You know what

might help you, take a look at the *Cyclone* again, the way a visual fabric is maintained even while the metaphor plays on different levels. Hey –

(nods to minivan)

This your ride, Chili?

Chili follows Martin over to the minivan, opens the door for him.

MARTIN: Very nice . . .

CHILI: Yeah, I like it, I'm high up, I can see everything, you know? It's the Cadillac of minivans.

MARTIN: What's that?

CHILI: Compass.

MARTIN: Wow.

(then)

Mind if I take it for a spin?

INT. ABIQUIU RESTAURANT – DAY

Bo Catlett and Harry are laughing as Harry, very drunk now finishes another drink . . .

BO CATLETT: He was watching Letterman, huh? Sneaky, that Chili Palmer.

(signals the waiter, then)

So, he ever find this dry cleaner, the one with all that money on him?

HARRY: Leo, I don't know.

Bo Catlett and the Bear look at each other.

BO CATLETT: I bet he did and he ain't givin' you a penny of it, help you out. Not the way I am.

Harry looks at Bo, can't believe what's happening to his life, thinks a moment, then . . .

HARRY: Assuming I go along with this, when can I have the five hundred?

BO CATLETT: Whenever you want it. The money's in hundred dollar bills inside one of those jock bags, you know? In a locker at the airport, waiting to be picked up.

HARRY: The *airport.*

BO CATLETT: It was waiting out there on another deal, one that didn't go through; one you don't want to know about.

Harry shakes his head, looks around the restaurant. Bo and the Bear exchange looks, then . . .

HARRY: I don't know.

BO CATLETT: It's not the kind of thing you do.

Another glance at the Bear, then . . .

BO CATLETT: That's why I was thinking you could send your boy Chili Palmer. He gets busted or hit on the head you aren't out nothing.

And with that, Bo Catlett calmly slides an ORANGE KEY across the table to Harry. Harry stares at it. It has the number C-18 printed on the flat orange part.

HARRY: C-18.

BO CATLETT: That's the magic number.

BEAR: Cat . . .

And they all look . . .

DOWNSTAIRS

as Chili and Karen enter the restaurant. Chili checks out the bar, sees they aren't there, then looks up at the railing . . . keeps his eyes up there as he says . . .

CHILI: Wait here.

Chili moves to the staircase, now sees the Bear in his Hawaiian shirt standing a few steps from the top.

Chili gets within three steps of the guy and stops, but doesn't look up, keeps his eyes fixed on the man's gut.

BO CATLETT: I'd like you to meet my associate, the Bear. Movie stuntman and champion weight-lifter, as you might've noticed. Picks up and throws out things I don't want.

Chili doesn't move, keeps his eyes on the man's crotch.

BEAR: We think you ought to turn around and go back to Miami.

Chili slowly moves his gaze up through hibiscus until he's looking at the man's bearded face . . .

CHILI: So you're a stuntman. Are you any good?

The Bear grins and turns his head to the side, as if too modest to answer and will let Bo Catlett speak for him.

This makes the next move easier . . . the guy not even looking as Chili grabs a handful of his crotch, steps aside and yanks him off the fucking stairs.

The Bear yells out of pain and fear as the beefy guy rolls all the way down the stairs to land on the main floor, a few feet away from where Karen now stands.

Chili keeps watching until he sees the guy move, then looks up at Bo Catlett who's now coming down . . .

CHILI: Not bad for a guy his size.

Chili continues up the stairs to where Bo Catlett stands beside the table. Chili unbuttons his coat . . .

CHILI: I'll make you a deal. If you can get out of here before I take my coat off, I won't clean the floor with you, get your little costume all messed up.

Karen watches now as Bo Catlett puts a hand in his coat pocket, steps right up to Chili . . .

BO CATLETT: You don't know me. You only think you do.

Bo walks past Chili, goes down the stairs. Chili watches as Bo Catlett helps the Bear get to his feet. They leave the restaurant, the Bear looking over his shoulder at Chili.

Even Karen is looking at him differently now as they slide into the booth with a now shocked, rapidly sobering Harry.

CHILI: Rough business this movie business. I may have to go back to loan sharking for a rest.

Harry doesn't say anything. Karen looks at him.

KAREN: Harry, what're you still doing with those guys?

HARRY: He happens to be loaning me five hundred grand, no strings, I write any kind of agreement I want.

CHILI: Is he giving you a check or cash?

HARRY: Cash. It happens to be waiting right at this moment in a locker at the airport.

KAREN: A locker at the airport? Jesus Christ, Harry. Tell me you're not really that stupid.

CHILI: The guy's setting you up. You pulled out of their *Freaks* deal so he's paying you back.

HARRY: Oh, is that right? I'm being set up? Then how come Catlett said I should send *you* out to get it, since you haven't done a fucking thing for me since you got into this . . . except showing Bo Catlett my script?

Chili looks at Karen, smiles, shakes his head . . .

CHILI: Okay, Harry, I'm wrong. You're not the one he's setting up.

HARRY: I mean, at least Bo's invested in three of my movies.

KAREN: Harry, we spoke with Martin.

HARRY: 'We?'

KAREN: Chili and me.

Harry looks at the two of them, differently now . . .

HARRY: Really.

CHILI: Yeah, he wants us to talk to Buddy, set up a meeting.

HARRY: A meeting with who? You and Karen?

KAREN: Harry –

HARRY: Man's in town two days, thinks he's David O.fucking Selznick.

Karen and Chili look at each other as Harry finishes his drink.

HARRY: So how 'bout it, Mr. Selznick, do I make my deal with Bo? Or you gonna finally help me out, have a word with your dry cleaner when you find him.

CHILI: I found him.

Harry looks at him.

CHILI: Forget about Leo's money, Harry.

HARRY: You have it?

CHILI: Harry, if I gave you Leo's money you'd have Ray Bones all over your ass and then you'd be in a whole new kinda trouble.

HARRY: Who?

CHILI: Ray Barboni. Guy from Miami, owns Leo now that Momo died.

HARRY: Who the fuck is Momo? Jesus, these fucking names . . .

CHILI: Tell you what, Harry, tomorrow morning, when the airport's crowded, I'll go check it out. If I don't see a problem, I'll pick up the money . . .

KAREN: I wouldn't get my hopes up, Harry.

Harry thinks a moment, lays the key on the table, but keeps his hand on it.

HARRY: Maybe I oughta talk to this Ray Bones character myself. See if he wants to invest in *my* movie.

CHILI: Don't waste your time, Harry. The guy's not much of a movie fan. Now c'mon, gimme the key.

Harry finally lifts his hand.

EXT. HARRY'S OFFICE – NIGHT

A light on upstairs . . .

HARRY: *(V.O.)* Bones. B-O-N-E-S.

INT. HARRY'S OFFICE – SAME TIME

Harry sits at his desk, the phone cradled to his ear, a half-empty bottle of scotch in front of him.

OPERATOR: *(PHONE)* I show a 'Dem Bones Barbecue' in Dade County, but that's all.

HARRY: Oh. Wait a minute. That's not his real name. It's uh . . . uh . . . yeah – try Barboni. B-a-rb-o-n-i.

INT. RAY BONES' APARTMENT – NIGHT

We start CLOSE ON A TELEPHONE . . . THE PHONE RINGS and we BOOM UP to reveal a CLOSED DOOR across the room . . .

INT. BATHROOM – SAME TIME

Ray Bones nests on the can, humming off key, reading Weir'D Tales, *Martin Weir's autobiography. He looks up, listens to the PHONE RING.*

BONES: Fuck.

The phone KEEPS RINGING. Bones thinks about it a moment, then tosses the book aside . . .

BONES: Fuck fuck fuck fuck . . .

INT. FRONT ROOM – SAME TIME

As Bones bursts out of the john and grabs the phone.

BONES: *What?*

INTERCUTTING HARRY & RAY BONES

Phone to his ear, Harry downs another drink, sits up.

HARRY: Ray Barboni?

BONES: Who is this?

HARRY: Are you the guy they called Ray Bones?

BONES: Depends. Who's this?

HARRY: Who is this? I'm the one telling you the

way it is, okay, asshole? That's who I am. Now you want your three hundred grand or don't you?

BONES: What three hundred grand?

HARRY: The three hundred grand a guy named Leo Devoe scammed off an airline. The three hundred grand Chili Palmer now has in his possession.

Okay. This gets Bones' attention.

HARRY: Hello? You there?

BONES: Yeah, I'm here. I just don't like the anonymous crap. It means your either chickenshit or not for real.

HARRY: Yeah? Well, trust me. I'm *very* for real.

BONES: Okay. So who are you?

HARRY: I work for Harry Zimm, alright?

BONES: Who?

HARRY: Harry Zimm. The man happens to be a major Hollywood player.

BONES: Never heard of him.

HARRY: Maybe that's because you've never been out've fuckin' Miami, dipshit. Maybe it's time you got on a plane, flew out to L.A. and took a meeting with Mr. Zimm.

Bones sits down, trying to put this together . . .

BONES: So, what, this Zimm guy asking for some

kinda finders fee, that what we're talking about here?

HARRY: Hey, Zimm doesn't *ask* for dick. Zimm *tells* you the way it is . . . or else.

BONES: Or else what?

HARRY: Or else use your fucking imagination.

Harry hangs up at the other end. Bones stares at the phone.

CONTINUED: INT. HARRY'S OFFICE – SAME TIME

He sits there a moment, also staring at the phone.

HARRY: Motherfucker.

He then realizes his hands are shaking, grabs the bottle and pours the rest of the scotch down his throat.

EXT. LAX – SOVEREIGN TERMINAL – MORNING

Busy. Travelers moving along the sidewalk. Here comes Chili . . . he enters the terminal and we . . .

INT. SOVEREIGN TERMINAL – DAY

CUT TO: A ROW OF LOCKERS

All with keys sticking out of them except one. We push in on that one . . . C-18.

CHILI

stands between rows of lockers on either side of him. He

studies them a moment longer, then looks up at the ARRIVALS MONITOR. He starts writing something on a CARD as we push past him . . . pushing in on #83 from NEWARK . . .

INT. AIRPORT GIFT SHOP – DAY

As Chili buys an L.A. LAKERS T-SHIRT and a BLACK CANVAS ATHLETIC BAG. He pauses to check out the magazine rack, Martin Weir is on the cover of everything including his hardback autobiography "WEIR'D TALES" He grabs a copy . . .

Chili puts the book and the T-shirt inside the athletic bag, puts that inside the paper gift shop bag, and then looks around . . .

A SCRUFFY LOOKING KID

Eighteen or so, checking out the skin magazines as Chili comes up behind him.

CHILI: You want to make five bucks, take you two minutes?

The kid looks at him, but doesn't answer.

CHILI: You go over to those lockers over there and put this in C–17.

The kid still doesn't say anything.

CHILI: It's a surprise for my wife. But you have to do it quick, okay? While she's in the can.

That sounds like it makes sense, so the kid nods . . .

KID: Yeah, okay.

Chili gives him the paper bag with his purchases, a five dollar bill and three quarters. He watches as . . .

The kid walks over to the row of lockers . . . puts the quarters into C-17, opens it, puts the stuff inside, pulls the key and then walks back over to Chili, and hands him the key . . .

CHILI: Thanks.

EXT. AIRPORT – DAY

As a plane touches down . . .

INT. SOVEREIGN TERMINAL – DAY

As Chili watches the last few passengers come off the plane. He watches them come through the gate until he's standing there by himself.

Okay, he turns and walks down the aisle now to the bank of lockers three high where C-18 is just about in the middle.

He looks both ways, takes his time until a group of people pass behind, giving him a screen, giving him just time enough to open C-17, grab the black athletic bag, and close the locker.

Chili gets about ten yards down the aisle, heading for daylight, when a BLACK GUY IN A SUIT comes towards him and stops right in his path . . .

BLACK GUY/CURTIS: Excuse me, sir . . .

Now there's a BIG GUY IN A PLAID WOOL SHIRT next to him, the same guy we saw when Bo

Catlett was here. And Christ, ANOTHER GUY now, this one down the aisle, talking on his hand radio. The Black Guy has his I.D. folder open . . .

BLACK GUY/CURTIS: Curtis. Drug Enforcement. These are Agents Dunbar and Morgan, would you come with us, please?

CHILI: What's wrong? What's this about?

Agent Curtis turns and starts off.

DUNBAR: Let's follow him and behave ourselves. What do you say?

As Chili walks off with the D.E.A. guys we see . . .

RAY BONES

Coming out one of the gates. He looks at A GUY holding a square piece of cardboard that reads MR. BARBONE.

GUY: Mr. Barbone? Welcome to L.A. I'm Bobby, your driver. You have a good flight?

RAY BONES: *(starts walking)* I hope you drive better than you fucking spell, jackoff. My name's Barboni, not Bar-bone.

As Ray Bones then walks off, we see coming out a different gate . . .

THREE COLOMBIANS

All in dark suits. Two big guys in sunglasses flanking one smaller, older guy . . .

BIG GUY: You want to go to the hotel first, Mr.

Escobar?

MR. ESCOBAR: I want to get my focking money.

INT. SMALL AIRPORT OFFICE – DAY

Chili stands there while Curtis opens Chili's wallet and looks at the driver's license while Dunbar in the plaid shirt pulls the Lakers T-shirt out of the athletic bag, feels around inside. The agents glance at each other without giving any kind of sign.

CURTIS: You live in Miami?

CHILI: That's right.

CURTIS: What're you doing in Los Angeles?

CHILI: I'm in the movie business.

CURTIS: You're an investor, is that it?

CHILI: I'm a producer.

CURTIS: You have a card in here?

CHILI: Not yet. I just started.

Chili watches Curtis pick up the note with the Newark Flight number and arrival time written on it.

CHILI: I'd appreciate your telling me what this is about.

MORGAN: I got a John Doe warrant here. I can strip-search you if I want.

CURTIS: Pat him down.

MORGAN: Why don't I strip-search him.

CURTIS: Pat him down.

The big guy puts Chili against the wall.

MORGAN: Spread your legs.

CURTIS: What're you doing at the airport?

CHILI: I was supposed to meet my wife, but she wasn't on the flight.

DUNBAR: Why, you live in Miami, was your wife coming from Newark?

CHILI: We had a fight and she left me, went back to Brooklyn. I asked her to come out here, you know, thinking with a change of scenery maybe we could get back together, and she said okay, but evidently she changed her mind.

CURTIS: Your wife a Lakers fan?

CHILI: I am. I'm a fan of everything that's L.A. I love it out here.

He looks over his shoulder to the give the guy a smile. Curtis doesn't return it.

CURTIS: You can go.

Chili moves to the table to collect his things. Curtis watches him then . . .

CURTIS: By the way, you recall the number of the locker you used?

CHILI: It was C . . . I don't know, sixteen or

seventeen, one of those. Why? You looking for anyway, a bomb or something?

CURTIS: Something shouldn't be there.

CHILI: Why don't you get the attendant to open all the lockers and take a look. Maybe you'll find it.

CURTIS: That's the idea. I'll think about it.

CHILI: That's what I'd do.

(looks right at Curtis)

Make sure I got the right guy next time.

CURTIS: Get him out've here.

EXT. FREEWAY – DAY

The usual L.A. traffic. A black caddy in the middle of it.

INT. CADDY – SAME TIME

As Ray Bones looks out a tinted window at the freeway.

BOBBY: You ever wanta go to the beach, here's the freeway you take we're coming to.

RAY BONES: I live in Miami and you want to show me a fuckin' beach? The sun ever come out here, or you have this smog all the time?

BOBBY: They say the smog's the reason we have such beautiful sunsets.

RAY BONES: That's what they say, huh? What a buncha fuckin' bullshit.

EXT. AIRPORT PARKING STRUCTURE –

DAY

Chili glances about, makes sure no one's around, then pulls the key for the 'right' locker out from a crack in the pavement, near the stairwell. He then goes up the stairs to . . .

EXT. AIRPORT PARKING STRUCTURE – DAY

ANOTHER LEVEL

where the Bear, in his trademark Hawaiian shirt is standing beside Chili's car. He straightens up as Chili exits the stairwell and walks up to him.

CHILI: I don't know how I could've missed you with that shirt on. It's the same as the other one you had only the hibiscus are a different color. Right?

BEAR: So you didn't have the key with you.

CHILI: You think I'd be standing here? You set somebody up and you want it to work, it has to be a surprise. Can you remember that?

BEAR: You spotted them, huh?

Chili looks at him, the guy's either dumb or making conversation.

CHILI: What, did you see it work in some movie you got beat up in?

BEAR: I have to ask you for that key.

CHILI: What, the setup didn't work so you want the key back?

BEAR: Catlett says if you don't open the locker the deal's off.

CHILI: You serious? This is how you guys do business? I can't believe you aren't dead.

The Bear keeps staring, but doesn't say anything.

CHILI: Look, there's no fuckin' way I'm gonna give you the key, outside of you point a gun at my head. Then we might have something to talk about. Now step away from the car.

BEAR: I don't need a gun. Where is it? If it isn't on you, it's around here someplace.

Chili shakes his head, tired of this, but still feeling a little sorry for the guy. He looks off in a kind of thoughtful way, turns to the Bear again and kicks him in the left knee, hard.

The Bear stumbles, hunching over. Chili grabs him by the hair with both hands, pulls his head down and brings his own knee up into the guy's face. This straightens him and now Chili hits him high in the belly as hard as he can, right under the rib cage.

The Bear sucks air with his mouth open trying to breathe, helpless now and in pain. Chili takes him by the arm . . .

CHILI: Lie down on your back. Come on, if you want to breathe.

He gets the Bear down on the concrete, straddles his midsection and reaches down to lift him up by the waist of his pants.

CHILI: Take deep breaths through your mouth and let it out slow . . . that's it, like that.

The Bear starts to breathe okay again. He checks his teeth now, feeling his nose . . .

CHILI: Hey, Bear, look at me.

The Bear looks at him.

CHILI: Tell your boss I don't ever want to see him again. He made a deal with Harry and a deal's a deal.

The Bear nods, closing and opening his eyes.

CHILI: What're you hanging around with a guy like that for? You were in the movies, right? A stuntman? What's *he* ever done he can talk about? You feel okay?

BEAR: Not too bad.

CHILI: How 'bout when you went down the stairs?

The Bear touches his thigh . . .

BEAR: I think I pulled my quadriceps.

CHILI: So . . . how many movies you been in?

BEAR: About sixty.

CHILI: No shit? What're some of 'em?

INT. HARRY'S OFFICE – DAY

Harry is passed out with his head on the blotter when we hear someone POUND ON THE DOOR. He jerks upright.

VOICE: Harry Zimm?

HARRY: What – who is it . . . ?

Harry, his hair a mess from sleeping on it, looks up at the door as it opens to reveal Ray Bones standing there.

RAY BONES: The dipshit who's never been out've Miami.

Harry wakes up quick, nearly wets himself as Bones then casually steps into the office.

HARRY: Mr. Barboni. Well. This is surprise . . .

Scrambling now to play it the way Chili taught him, Harry quickly gestures to the red leather chair across the desk.

HARRY: Please. Have a seat. Right here in this chair right here . . .

As Ray Bones sits down, Harry moves to the blinds and opens them. Problem is, the sun's setting, so there's no glare at all. Ray indicates the nice red sunset . . .

BONES: They say the fuckin' smog's the reason you have such beautiful sunsets.

Harry just smiles, sits down at the desk, things already not going too well, about to get worse . . .

INT. WINGATE MOTORS OFFICE – SAME TIME

The walls are covered with posters of Porsches and Ferraris, the kind you can buy at the carwash with severely titted chicks sprawled on the hoods. Bo Catlett is behind a big wooden desk on the phone.

BO CATLETT: Whatta you mean, he faked them out?

EXT. AIRPORT PAYPHONE – DAY

The Bear, sort of half doubled over . . .

BEAR: He knew it was a set up. He was ready for it.

INTERCUTTING BO CATLETT & THE BEAR:

BO CATLETT: So where's the money?

BEAR: I guess still in the locker.

BO CATLETT: You guess? You mean you don't know?

BEAR: I mean I don't care.

Bo Catlett looks into the outer office as a car pulls into the garage. Three dark-shaded gentlemen step out of the car.

BO CATLETT: Bear, I'm going to call you later.

INT. WINGATE MOTORS OFFICE – DAY

Bo Catlett hangs up, gets to his feet as the men all look into the office now.

BO CATLETT: Mr. Escobar. What a surprise. Welcome to L.A.

We can now see that one of the Latinos is older, the other two, younger, are his bodyguards. Mr. ESCOBAR, the older, meaner one . . . steps into the office . . .

ESCOBAR: Where is my nephew?

BO CATLETT: Your who?

ESCOBAR: Yayo. Where is he?

Bo Catlett stiffens . . . Uh oh.

INT. GARAGE – DAY

As the two back doors of a limo slam shut. There's half dozen other limos wedged in here.

INT. LIMO – SAME TIME

Bo Catlett sits in the back, wedged in between the two bodyguards, neither of whom has removed his shades. He faces Escobar on the opposite seat.

ESCOBAR: He's my sister's kid. No papa. Not too bright. Personally, I think he's a retard. I only gave him the job as a favor for my sister, you understand?

BO CATLETT: Sure. Family. I know how that goes.

ESCOBAR: He comes up here with our product. He suppose to come home with five hundred thousand dollars. He never shows up. Meanwhile, my sister's going crazy calling me all the time worried about him. Me, I just wanna know what happened to my focking money.

BO CATLETT: Well, I don't know. I gave the

man his money, sent him on his way.

ESCOBAR: You gave him the money?

BO CATLETT: I gave him a key to a locker that had the money in it.

ESCOBAR: Now why would you do that? Put the money in a locker?

BO CATLETT: Because there were a zillion DEA guys hanging around the terminal.

ESCOBAR: *(flat)* A zillion, huh? That's a lot.

Escobar studies him a moment. Bo Catlett shrugs.

BO CATLETT: Maybe your nephew panicked, took off.

ESCOBAR: Where's your partner, the jumpy one? Why isn't he here?

BO CATLETT: He's around someplace.

ESCOBAR: I hear he's around Palm Springs. Dealing our product. Product we sold to you for five hundred thousand dollars.

(then)

Why do you keep talking to me bullshit? I think maybe I have Ramon and Ceasar staple your tongue to your chin. What do you think?

Bo Catlett barely glances at the bodyguards, smiles the gleamy smile to the Latin guy in front of him . . .

BO CATLETT: You know, you speak very good

English, Mr. Escobar.

ESCOBAR: I went to UC San Diego.

(then)

We're gonna spend the weekend at the Universal Sheraton. We're gonna take the tour. See the shark. Check out the Miami Vice Action Spectacular. After, we'll come here, get our money.

One of the bodyguards says 'Your nephew' in Spanish.

ESCOBAR: Oh, yeah, and Yayo, too.

INT. RONNIE WINGATE'S PORSCHE – DAY

As Ronnie zigzags in and out of traffic, giving people the 'look' as he passes . . . on the carphone.

RONNIE: His fucking nephew?

INT. WINGATE MOTORS – SAME TIME

Bo Catlett on the phone . . .

BO CATLETT: You get to town, you go straight to the bank, raid the limo account.

INTERCUTTING RONNIE & BO CATLETT:

RONNIE: I'm already in town, but it don't matter. We got dick in the bank. We dumped it all in Harry's movie.

BO CATLETT: What I'm sayin' is the man wants his money and he wants it now.

INT. HARRY'S OFFICE – DAY

Ray Bones impatiently listening to Harry . . .

HARRY: I'm talking about you, Ray Barboni, owning a piece of a major motion picture. How big a piece is up to you. What I'm saying, you could invest part of the three hundred Palmer owes you or you could invest all of it. It's entirely up to you . . .

Bones leans forward . . .

BONES: Where's Leo Devoe? Where's Chili Palmer? *Where's my fuckin' money?*

HARRY: Ray. Look at me.

Uh-oh . . . Ray's heard that one before . . .

BONES: What?

HARRY: Look at me, Ray.

BONES: You say look at you?

HARRY: That's correct. Look at me.

Bones shakes his head, stands up . . .

BONES: I tell you what . . .

And in one fast move, Ray Bones grabs the phone off the desk and slams it into Harry Zimm's surprised face . . .

BONES: Fuckin look at *that*, asshole . . .

Bones then yanks the phone out of the wall and throws it down at Harry . . .

BONES: And have a peek at *that* . . .

Ray Bones pulls a pair of black leather gloves from his

pocket and steps around the desk . . . begins kicking the living shit out of Harry Zimm . . .

BONES: You know, Harry, this is the exact fucking thing I needed after the fucking plane flight. My ass fell asleep . . .

(kick)

. . . seven times. I need a little fucking . . .

(kick)

. . . exercise.

Harry tries to push himself to his feet, but Ray Bones stomps on Harry's hands . . . breaking them . . . and Harry falls back down . . . Bones crouches down . . .

BONES: You got a big problem, Harry.

Bones grabs him by the hair, picks him up and throws him across the room into the wall of pictures, many of them coming off their hooks and falling on top of Harry.

BONES: Hey, Harry . . . *Harry.* Don't you pass out on me. Look up here . . .

Harry, a crumpled heap, looks up and we see his bloody pummeled face as Ray Bones quickly crosses the room. He steps on Harry's neck with his shoe, pinning him to the floor . . .

BONES: Where's my money?

Harry can't speak; his jaw is broken. He looks sad lying there pinned beneath Ray Bones' shoe, wondering how it all went so wrong.

Bones pulls a 9mm from his coat pocket and aims it down at Harry's face . . .

BONES: Harry. I'm gonna ask you one more time, then I'm gonna shoot you, you don't tell me what I wanna know . . .

Harry just makes a noise. Bones aims the gun at him.

BONES: Where's my money?

VOICE: *Your* money?

Ray Bones looks over as Ronnie Wingate strolls into the office . . . Harry actually looks glad to see him.

RONNIE: Who the fuck are you?

BONES: Ray Barboni. From Miami.

RONNIE: What, like that's supposed to mean something to me?

Ronnie then puts a cigarette in his mouth, eyes Bones. Harry tries to follow what's happening from the floor.

RONNIE: The man you're steppin' on belongs to me and my partner.

BONES: He owes me money.

RONNIE: Get in line, bro.

BONES: I don't like waiting.

RONNIE: Tough shit, bro. This ain't Miami. You want something, talk to me.

BONES: Hey, fuckball, I don't need your

permission. L.A.'s an open city.

Ronnie opens his jacket so that Ray Bones can see the .357 Ronnie's got tucked into his belt.

RONNIE: Yeah, well, I just closed it.

Bones looks at the gun, looks up at Ronnie standing there, hands on his hips, holding his jacket open. Bones raises his own gun . . .

BONES: You a quick draw . . . 'bro?' You better be, your piece stuck way down in your belt like that.

RONNIE: Whatta you got there . . . some kinda pop nine, the fuckin' Fiat of guns, always jammin' at the wrong time.

Okay. Bones thinks about that. His confidence a little shaken. They stand there a moment. Harry raises his hand, makes a gurgling noise as . . .

Ronnie goes for his gun.

Boom. Boom. Boom. Harry closes his eyes as Ray Bones shoots Ronnie over and over, knocking the guy backwards until he hits the door, and slumps to the floor.

Ray Bones stares at Ronnie a moment, then comes out of his trance, looks down . . . quickly steps back . . .

BONES: Don't you puke on my shoes, Harry.

Harry rolls over on to his side. Ray Bones deep in thought now, picks the telephone up off the floor, sets it back down on the desk, then looks at Ronnie again.

BONES: Harry. I need you to do me a favor . . .

Harry rolls over and looks up at Ray Bones.

BONES: I need you to take this gun and put a pill in the bro over there for me.

Harry looks at the dead Ronnie Wingate, slumped up against the door, staring vacantly back at him.

BONES: I know what you're thinking, 'Why the fuck would I shoot him? He's already dead.'

Ray Bones crouches down beside him. Harry winces as Ray puts the gun in Harry's broken hand.

BONES: But see, the cops got these tests, tell them whether or not a person fired a gun. And I was never here.

Harry looks pleadingly at Ray Bones.

BONES: You understand, Harry? I was never here. You say I was, and I'm gonna come back here throw you out that fuckin' window.

Harry looks at the gun, feebly aims it at Bones. Bones frowns, pushes the gun away . . .

BONES: C'mon, knock it off, Harry. We don't have a lotta time here . . .

Harry looks up at Ronnie, raises the gun . . .

EXT. KAREN'S BACKYARD – DUSK

Beer in hand, Chili sits in a chaise longue by the pool. Karen watches him a moment from the doorway . . .

KAREN: Not a worry in the world.

He looks over . . .

CHILI: Your pool needs skimming.

She comes over, sits down.

KAREN: That was Martin. He wants to have lunch tomorrow. That is, if you can make it.

CHILI: Depends, who pays?

KAREN: Definitely not Martin. Movie stars never pick up the check. They have no idea what things cost. Most of them don't know their zip code and a lot don't even know their own phone number.

Chili looks at Karen a moment.

CHILI: How'd you meet Martin anyway?

KAREN: Not unlike the way Nicki met him. Except it was a wrap party. Why?

CHILI: I don't know, I'm just havin' some trouble seeing you two together.

KAREN: You don't like Martin much, do you?

CHILI: Oh, I like him. I just think he's . . . short. I mean, he's a good actor and all, but I'm wondering what it was exactly you saw in Marty.

KAREN: For starters, Marty wasn't Martin back then.

Feeling him staring, she keeps her eyes on the sunset, and tries to change the subject . . .

KAREN: So what about your story. You thought of a title yet?

CHILI: How 'bout *Get Martin*? Except that isn't a movie. That's real life.

KAREN: How 'bout *Chili's Hollywood Adventure*.

CHILI: That's a different story. I'm still working on that one, you know, getting the visual fabric just right.

(then)

Although I've added to it.

He looks at her, puts his drink down.

KAREN: Yeah?

CHILI: Yeah. There's a girl in it now.

KAREN: Really.

And he leans over and kisses her.

INT. KAREN'S BEDROOM – NIGHT

Karen and Chili lie in bed together. She looks at him . . .

KAREN: I think you could be an actor. I know you're acting sometimes, but you don't show it.

CHILI: You thought I was faking?

KAREN: No. I don't mean *that*. I just meant in general.

CHILI: Oh.

They're both quiet for a moment. Then . . .

CHILI: You don't mean a movie star? More like a character actor?

KAREN: Whichever. Let's talk about it tomorrow.

But Chili can't stop thinking about this now . . .

CHILI: I mean I could see myself in movies Robert De Niro had been in. Or I could maybe do an Al Pacino movie, play a hard-on. But I couldn't see myself in ones, like say the one where the three guys get stuck with a baby. They don't know how to take care of it and you see these big grown-up assholes acting cute –

KAREN: Hey, Chili? Look at me.

She leans over and kisses him. Is still kissing him when the PHONE RINGS. They ignore it, let things heat up as we hear the ANSWERING MACHINE pick up O.S. . . .

KAREN: *(V.O.)* I'm not in right now. Leave a message at the beep . . .

A BEEP, followed by . . .

DORIS: *(V.O.)* Hi, Karen. It's Doris. Listen, doll, you might wanna come by Cedars tonight and visit Harry. He's in the emergency room . . .

Chili and Karen both jerk upright.

INT. EMERGENCY ROOM – SAME TIME

As Doris leads Karen and Chili towards the triage area.

DORIS: I stopped by his office to see if he wanted to take me to Le Dome for dinner when I saw Harry and this other man lying on the floor.

Doris smiles as two UNIFORMED COPS walk past.

DORIS: Goodnight, Todd. Night, Louis.

Karen and Chili exchange a look as they follow her into . . .

THE TRIAGE AREA

Where Harry lies in bed in a pain-killer stupor. Both of his eyes are black. His face is swollen and purple.

KAREN: Harry . . . My God . . .

CHILI: What happened?

He raises a bandaged hand and waves feebly . . .

DORIS: He can't talk. He's full of Demerol.

Harry tries to pull away as she runs a hand through his hair.

CHILI: Who'd he shoot?

DORIS: According to Todd – Sergeant Randall – a man named Ronnie came by Harry's office to collect on a debt. He got rough and Harry shot him.

CHILI: You shot one of the limo guys?

Harry gives Chili a sad look. We then hear . . .

VOICE: Hello, hello . . .

They all look over as a RESIDENT walks over trailed by

several MED STUDENTS.

RESIDENT: *(enthusiastic)* Okay . . . here we go. Looks like Mr. Zimm here's got a broken jaw and some neck trauma to go with those fractured hands . . .

Doris winks at one of the young med students as the resident then turns to her, Karen, Chili.

RESIDENT: Excuse me, folks . . .

They step back as the Resident pulls the curtain shut, blocking their view of Harry.

KAREN: Hey, Harry, listen, Martin wanted to meet us tomorrow at the Ivy for lunch. I'd cancel, but Martin's going to Cannes next week, so I think maybe Chili and I should still go.

We hear HARRY GRUNT from behind the curtain, then . . .

RESIDENT: *(O.S.)* Okay, who wants to take a crack at wiring Mr. Zimm's jaw?

Chili and Karen look at each other as we then . . .

DISSOLVE TO:

ext. BO'S DECK – MORNING

A PHOTOGRAPH OF HARRY ZIMM

Standing beside some giant mutant maggot or something. We begin PULLING BACK . . . now we can read a headline above the photograph, 'PRODUCER INVOLVED IN SHOOTING.'

BO CATLETT: *(V.O.)* Motherfucker . . .

As Bo Catlett sits on his deck reading the newspaper. From inside, we hear the front door open and a moment later, the Bear steps out on to the deck, with Farrah, his little girl.

BO CATLETT: Mother*fucker* . . .

Bo Catlett looks over as Bear CLEARS HIS THROAT, indicates Farrah . . .

BO CATLETT: Hey, Bear. I been calling you, man. Where you been?

FARRAH: Hi Bo.

BO CATLETT: Hey, Farrah. Hah you, little honey bunny. You wipe your feet, for you come in here? Keep Uncle Bo's carpet nice and white.

BEAR: You see the paper?

BO CATLETT: I seen it, but I don't believe it. Says Harry shot Ronnie five times. Four to the chest and one through his foot.

BEAR: His foot. Jeez, poor Ronnie . . .

BO CATLETT: Yeah, I'm really gonna miss him.

Bo throws the paper aside.

BO CATLETT: Listen, tonight, later on, I got one for you doesn't involve any heavy work. I want you to go have a look around Chili Palmer's hotel room.

BEAR: I can't. I got to take Farrah to Satan's place

down in Costa Mesa.

BO CATLETT: Who?

BEAR: Her mother. Not that it matters because I don't work for you no more. I quit. I just wanted to come by, tell you to your face so there's no misunderstanding.

BO CATLETT: Whoa . . . This is the man used to jump offa high buildings?

BEAR: Into air bags. There's no cushion under what you're doing. I'm out of it, Cat. I'm done.

BO CATLETT: Bear. The Colombians are in L.A. Seems they all upset about their money. That ain't enough, as a bonus, it turns out the yoyo was Escobar's nephew.

BEAR: That's your problem. You shouldn't've smoked the guy.

Bo Catlett looks at the Bear, then smiles at Farrah . . .

BO CATLETT: Come here, honey bunny, come sit with your Uncle Bo. He hates being alone.

Bear watches uncomfortably as Farrah sits down with Bo. Bo looks up at the Bear . . .

BO CATLETT: Fact, he hates it so much, if he takes a fall, he ain't gonna fall by himself.

Bo Catlett keeps his mouth close to her ear . . .

BO CATLETT: He's gonna plea-deal his way out. Give up this ace stunt man now one of the West

Coast dope kings, if they go easy on the Cat.

BEAR: Come here, Farrah . . .

Bo Catlett holds on to her, looks up at the Bear.

BO CATLETT: I heard in the Federal joints they let you spend an extra five minutes at the glass with your Daddy on Father's Day.

BEAR: *Farrah. Come here.*

Farrah slips off the couch, walks over to the Bear . . .

BEAR: After this one, I'm out, Cat, you understand? This is the last time we talk to each other.

BO CATLETT: Remember Harry's story about the dry cleaner Palmer was after? Guy who stole the three hundred grand from the airline?

BEAR: What about him?

BO CATLETT: I was thinking tonight you could go have a look around Palmer's hotel room while I go check out Karen Flores' place. See if he hasn't stashed it somewhere.

BEAR: *(beat)* And if we don't happen to find it under Palmer's mattress or inside Karen Flores' undie drawer? What then?

BO CATLETT: Just do what I told you and meet me back here at midnight.

And he winks at Farrah.

EXT. KAREN'S HOUSE – DAY

Chili's minivan is parked out front.

VOICE: *(V.O.)* Sunset Marquis.

INT. KAREN'S HOUSE – SAME TIME

Chili, dressed in his suit, on the phone.

CHILI: This is Mr. Palmer. I have any messages.

HOTEL OPERATOR: *(PHONE)* A Tommy Carlo called. He said to tell you that a Mr. Barboni was on his way to Los Angeles and that you should . . .

(clears throat)

. . . get the fuck out of there.

CHILI: When was this?

OPERATOR: Two nights ago.

Chili hangs up as Karen comes into the room wearing a black suit, no blouse underneath, putting on an earring.

CHILI: Wow. Nice earrings.

EXT. KAREN'S HOUSE – DAY

As Karen and Chili walk out to the minivan . . .

CHILI: What kinda food they serve at this Ivy place anyway?

KAREN: Continental, but it doesn't matter. Martin won't order from the menu.

He opens the door for her . . .

CHILI: Why not?

KAREN: Because a movie star can never order straight from the menu. They have to think of something they have to have that *isn't on* the menu.

EXT. THE IVY – DAY

As the valet drives off with Chili's minivan, a CAB pulls up and Harry – his hands bandaged, his neck in a massive brace – gets out . . .

KAREN: Harry, what're you doing? You're supposed to be in the hospital.

CHILI: Yeah, Harry, you look like you belong in one of your horror movies.

Harry waves them off, points to himself as he mumbles through his wired jaw . . .

HARRY: . . . my project . . .

He then pushes past them and limps up the steps. The hubub on the patio quiets as the three of them then walk up to the Maitre D'.

INT. THE IVY – DAY

MAITRE D': Mr. Zimm. Nice to see you.

Harry looks at him, not used to being greeted like this.

MAITRE D': Right this way.

All eyes are on Harry as they're led to a table. Karen sits down, looks about at all of the gawking diners . . .

KAREN: You're a celebrity, Harry. You shoulda shot someone a long time ago.

Chili watches Harry try to shake a cigarette out of the pack. Chili reaches over and helps him out.

CHILI: Tell me, Harry, what'd you think of Ray Bones as a person?

Harry goes stiff, looks at Chili as he lights one for himself . . .

CHILI: Only a guy like Bones would mess you up like this, break your hands for no reason. He shoot Ronnie, too?

Harry looks at Karen, quickly looks away.

CHILI: Thing I don't get, Harry, is why'd you go and do a thing like talking to Ray Bones. You don't need guys like him or Bo Catlett.

Harry looks at Chili now.

CHILI: I been here a while now and far as I can tell you're the only person in town actually making a movie instead of just talking about it.

Before Harry can answer, we hear a murmur and Chili and Karen look across the patio to the street, where . . .

EXT. THE IVY – DAY

MARTIN WEIR

gets out of a NEW MINIVAN, exactly like Chili's rental.

INT. THE IVY – DAY

We PAN WITH Martin as he stops off to say hello to people sticking their hands out at him to greet him, laugh at his stupid jokes . . .

MARTIN: Chill. Harry.

Chili nods as Martin smiles, leans down and kisses Karen.

MARTIN: Hi, sweetface. You look great. And mmmmm, you smell good, too.

KAREN: Thanks.

Martin sits down and fans the air in front of him.

MARTIN: Would you guys mind terribly not smoking?

Chili takes another drag, blows it out past Martin. Harry stubs his out, doing the best he can with two broken hands.

MARTIN: So. Harry. I hear you had quite an experience.

Harry grunts.

MARTIN: Well, I'm glad you're okay. And you know what else?

Harry watches Karen and Chili a moment longer, turns to Martin . . .

MARTIN: I'm glad you rejected me ten years ago when I auditioned for Eddie Solomon, the pedophile clown in *Birthday Boy*. Had I gotten the part. I might've gotten typecast.

Martin smiles at his own joke, looks up as the Maitre D' approaches. Harry turns back to Chili and Karen.

MARTIN: You all ready to order? I kind've have another thing after this . . .

Chili watches anticipatingly as Martin studies the menu for maybe a second, returns it to the waiter . . .

MARTIN: You know, I feel like an omelette. You think I could have a cheese omelette with shallots, but with the shallots only slightly browned . . .

Karen and Chili exchange looks, pick up their menus.

DISSOLVE TO:

INT. THE IVY – DAY

They've finished lunch. Chili shares a bowl of ice cream with Karen. Harry sips cognac through one of those tiny cocktail straws . . .

MARTIN: I think the romance angle in your story is critically important, that isn't simply a jump in the sack for either of them. These two become deeply in love.

Harry looks up . . . mumbles through his wired jaw . . .

HARRY: Which two?

MARTIN: *(ignoring him)* Once their lives are in danger and you have the mob guy coming after them, it not only heightens the tension, it adds a wistful element to their love.

HARRY: Mob guy?

Harry touches his jaw. It hurts to speak.

MARTIN: I have to consider, I mean, as the mob guy, this is another man's wife I'm sleeping with.

KAREN: And after all, you have such morals.

Harry looks to Karen for help here . . .

HARRY: Mob guy?

Martin looks at his watch.

MARTIN: I have to run. But what I hope to see, they begin to have misgivings about wanting the money. It becomes their moral dilemma and they try to rationalize keeping it, but in the end they can't. Can they?

HARRY: What money?

MARTIN: *(bewildered)* The three hundred large. What other money is there?

(then)

I should keep quiet, I know, till I've read the script, but I've got a feeling about this one. I'm that shylock.

HARRY: *Shylock?*

Harry winces in pain. Martin turns to him . . .

MARTIN: Look at me, Harry.

Harry's already looking at him.

MARTIN: Whatta you think, Chill?

CHILI: That's not bad. I think you got it down.

Harry turns to Chili, and back to Martin again. Just now getting it . . .

MARTIN: Really, it scares me how well I know him. I could do this one tomorrow, no further preparation.

(to Karen)

Bye darlin' . . . you really should think about acting again. I mean, maybe we could even do something together.

Now Harry looks at Karen who forces a smile at Martin.

KAREN: I'll give it some heavy thought.

EXT. KAREN'S HOUSE – NIGHT.

No lights on. Chili's minivan out front.

KAREN: *(V.O.)* Chili. Wake up.

INT. KAREN'S BEDROOM – SAME TIME

Karen sits up in bed. Chili lies asleep beside her. She nudges him . . .

KAREN: Wake up. Someone's downstairs.

Chili sits up on his elbows, listens. We can hear the TV.

KAREN: It's Harry. Downstairs.

Chili sits up on his elbows, listens.

CHILI: You sure?

KAREN: He's doing the same thing you did to him, playing Letterman on TV.

CHILI: It's not Dave. It's a movie.

KAREN: Are you going down?

CHILI: I don't know.

KAREN: *(getting up)* You're as bad as Harry . . .

CHILI: I'll go. I'll go.

He gets up, pulls on his pants and the Lakers T-shirt he bought at the airport.

CHILI: Hey, Karen, you have a gun? Any kind would be fine.

She shakes her head. He listens to the TV, then . . .

CHILI: I think it's *Rio Bravo*.

INT. KAREN'S STUDY – SAME TIME

The big-screen TV on loud, the big .45 in his lap. This time it's a movie, a western, not David Letterman that's on. John Wayne and Dean Martin shooting bad guys as Chili steps into the doorway and looks around; the room is empty now. Chili moves to the television and turns the volume down . . .

He's about to walk out when the dark shape of Bo Catlett steps into the doorway and startles him . . .

BO CATLETT: I need the money.

CHILI: What money?

BO CATLETT: The three hundred grand you got from a little dry cleaner named Leo.

CHILI: Lemme see if I got this right, you break into Karen Flores' house, ask me for three hundred grand, doesn't even belong to you?

INT. KAREN'S HOUSE – HALLWAY

As Karen comes down the stairs, she can see Bo Catlett standing in the doorway bathed in the flickering light.

BO CATLETT: *(O.S.)* Give it to me, I'll be on my way.

INT. KAREN'S STUDY – SAME TIME

As Chili shakes his head at Bo Catlett . . .

CHILI: I can't believe the way you guys do business out here. I can't believe how fucked up your organization is.

BO CATLETT: Tell you what . . .

Bo Catlett raises the .45 . . .

BO CATLETT: How 'bout I give you to three, then I organize your fuckin' brains all over the wall back there. One . . .

CHILI: What, you gonna shoot me now, Bo?

BO CATLETT: In just a second. Two . . .

CHILI: I don't believe this.

BO CATLETT: Three.

Bo Catlett is about to fire . . . when we hear a SCREAM. Not just any scream, but a completely professional one that fills the house and is all over Bo Catlett so that he starts firing before he's ready, giving Chili time to dive out of the way as . . .

Bo Catlett begins firing all over the room . . . keeps on firing until without thinking he blows out the TV and the room goes dark and the scream stops. Then . . .

CHILI: *(V.O.)* Karen? You okay?

BO CATLETT: *(V.O.)* She can't talk right now.

We hear movement, then the lamp goes on and we see Chili standing beside the desk looking to the doorway where Bo Catlett now has his hand over Karen's mouth. She struggles, but Bo hangs on to her . . .

BO CATLETT: That's a nice scream, lady. You oughta be in movies.

CHILI: Alright, Bo. You can have the money . . . but it's not here. I have to go get it.

BO CATLETT: Okay. Fine. The meantime, I'll just hang on to her for safe keeping.

Chili and Karen are looking at each other now.

BO CATLETT: You know Laurel Canyon?

CHILI: I'll find it.

BO CATLETT: I'm at 8150 Wonderland Avenue. It's right off Laurel.

CHILI: *(looking at Karen)* Gimme an hour.

EXT. BO CATLETT'S HOUSE – NIGHT

As Bo Catlett pulls up, drags Karen out of the car.

INT. BO CATLETT'S HOUSE – SAME TIME

*The Bear gets up off the couch as Bo Catlett shoves Karen
inside . . .*

BO CATLETT: You get the money?

BEAR: No. What's this?

BO CATLETT: Plan B. Here ya go, honey . . .

*He shoves Karen into the bathroom and shuts the
door . . .*

BO CATLETT: Make yourself comfortable.

INT. BATHROOM – SAME TIME

As Karen shuts the door on him. She listens a moment.

BO CATLETT: We gonna make a little trade.

She spots a copy of Martin's hardback Weir'D Tales *by
the toilet.*

KAREN: For Christ sake . . .

INT. LIVING ROOM – SAME TIME

Bo Catlett goes over to the stereo.

BEAR: Trade for what?

BO CATLETT: The *money.* Fuck. I gotta
think . . .

We hear Marvin Gaye OVER . . .

BEAR: Jesus, Bo, what're you doing?

Karen sticks her head out the door . . .

KAREN: He doesn't know what the fuck he's doing.

Bo Catlett points the gun at her face . . .

BO CATLETT: Shut up.

She closes the door.

BEAR: So you kidnapped her?

Karen opens the door again . . .

KAREN: That's a fucking federal offense, asshole!

BEAR/BO CATLETT: Shut up!

Again she shuts the door.

BEAR: You get life for kidnapping.

BO CATLETT: Calm down, Bear . . .

BEAR: Calm down? We're going away for life and you tell me to calm down?

He taps Bo's gun . . .

BEAR: *(ranting)* Hell, why not just shoot her? Why not shoot everybody. Fuckin' shoot me. Shoot the fuckin' president?

BO CATLETT: Don't fade on me now, Bear. Not unless you wanna hold Farrah on your lap in a room fulla felons.

The two men stare at each as we hear . . .

INT. HOUSE – SAME TIME

CHILI: So this's one of those houses you see way up hanging over the cliff.

They both look over at Chili, standing in the doorway, lighting a cigarette.

CHILI: Where's Karen?

BO CATLETT: *(nods to the closed door)* In the can. That the money?

Chili opens Leo's bag so that Bo can see the money.

CHILI: Lemme see her.

Bo Catlett shrugs, walks over and opens the bathroom door. Karen stands there with her arms folded across her chest.

CHILI: You okay?

KAREN: Guy's got a fucking pink toilet, for Christ's sake.

BO CATLETT: She's great. Gimme the money.

CHILI: First you and me gotta get a couple things straight.

Chili walks to the doorway leading out to the deck and turns around. He eyes Bo Catlett a moment, then . . .

CHILI: I've been shot at before – once by accident, twice on purpose. I'm still here and I'm gonna be here as long as I want. That means you're gonna have to be somewhere else, not anywhere near me or Harry or Karen.

Chili sets the duffle bag down in front of him.

CHILI: Here's your money. Take it and leave the movie business to the rest of us, know what we're doing. C'mon Karen . . .

They turn to leave, we hear a LOUD CLICK as Bo raises the gun, takes a step towards them . . .

BO CATLETT: You broke in my house and I have a witness to it.

CHILI: *What?*

Chili looks at the Bear. The Bear won't look at him.

BO CATLETT: Only this time, no John Wayne and Dean Martin shooting the bad guys in *El Dorado*.

CHILI: It was *Rio Bravo*. Robert Mitchum was the drunk in *El Dorado*, Dean Martin in *Rio Bravo*, practically the same part. John Wayne, he also did the same thing in both. He played John Wayne.

BO CATLETT: Man, I can't wait for you to be dead.

CHILI: Bear, you're not really gonna –

The Bear hooks one to Chili's face. Chili drops to his knees.

BEAR: That's for the stairs.

The Bear kicks him, sending Chili back into the living room at Karen's feet.

BEAR: Ever fallen down stairs before? It really hurts . . .

KAREN: Hey –

Karen moves to help Chili. Bo raises the gun . . .

BO CATLETT: You wanna go first, honey? That's fine with me.

Bear picks up Chili . . .

BO CATLETT: Get him off my carpet, you gonna make him bleed like that.

The Bear knees Chili in the gut, then shoves him out on to the balcony. Bo Catlett follows them out there . . .

BO CATLETT: Like I say, 'I warned him, officer, but he kept coming at me . . .'

The Bear follows Chili out, hits him again.

BEAR: And that's for the airport.

BO CATLETT: Hey, he should have a weapon, a knife or something.

BEAR: We'll get it later.

And the Bear hits Chili again . . .

BO CATLETT: Okay, Bear . . . that's enough.

But the Bear can't stop, keeps hitting Chili. Bo moves up to the Bear . . .

BO CATLETT: Hey, Bear . . . enough!

The Bear looks at Bo Catlett . . .

BO CATLETT: You keep hittin' him like that, he ain't gonna look like he broke in anymore, he gonna look like someone beat him up and then shot him.

BEAR: You're right.

And then the Bear, holding on to the back of Chili's shirt, shoves him towards Bo Catlett, who takes a step back, and grabs the rail behind behind him, and drops the gun as he gets a funny look on his face as . . . THE RAIL BREAKS AWAY . . .

BO CATLETT: Fuck . . .

He flails a moment, grabbing at space, but then quickly grabs on to Chili . . .

CHILI: Hey –

The Bear tries to pull Chili back, but ends up holding a handful of Chili's shirt as both Chili and Bo Catlett go over the rail together and drop from sight . . .

KAREN: Chili!

EXT. FROM THE HOUSE BELOW – LOOKING UP AT BO CATLETT'S HOUSE

As a body falls . . . too dark to see who . . .

EXT. BO CATLETT'S DECK – SAME TIME

As Karen spots THE GUN on the deck as two hands

appear on the edge and the Bear rushes forward . . .

BEAR: C'mon, man, gimme your hand . . . we gotta get outta here . . .

Behind the Bear, Karen picks the gun up off the deck, points it at the Bear . . .

BEAR: Hey, Karen, don't –

The Bear reaches down again and BOOM! Karen SHOOTS THE BEAR IN THE LEG. He cries out, falls back and lets go of . . .

CHILI

Who now barely hangs on to the deck.

CHILI: Karen! What the fuck are you doing?!

KAREN: Oh, shit . . .I'm sorry . . . I thought that was . . . I'm so sorry . . .

She comes over to the edge . . . helps the now wounded Bear pull Chili back up on to the deck. Then they all stand there looking down at Bo Catlett lying in the weeds and scraggly bushes, a hundred or so feet down, not moving.

Marvin Gaye singing 'Ain't No Mountain High Enough' as Chili then steps back, looks at the railing . . .

CHILI: Jesus. How'd that happen?

The Bear starts taking bolts and nuts, old used ones, out of his pants pockets. Wiping each one on his shirt before dropping it over the side . . .

BEAR: Beats the shit out of me.

BO CATLETT'S POV – CHILI, KAREN, &
THE BEAR

*The three of them looking down. Slowly the picture gets
blurry as we then . . .*

FADE OUT.

We then TILT DOWN TO REVEAL:

EXT. SUNSET MARQUIS HOTEL – NIGHT

*As Chili and Karen pull to the curb out front. She looks
at him . . .*

KAREN: Were you scared up there?

CHILI: You bet.

KAREN: You don't act like it?

CHILI: I was scared then, not now. How long you
want me to be scared?

She looks off, shakes her head . . .

CHILI: I'll be right back.

KAREN: *(shakes her head)* Go get your stuff.

INT. CHILI'S ROOM – NIGHT

*As Chili enters, takes off his suitcoat, drapes it over a
chair. He takes his suitcase out of the closet, throws it on
the bed, and freezes as . . .*

RAY BONES

extending the 9mm at Chili, comes out of the bathroom.

CHILI: You don't need that. You want to sit down and talk, it's fine with me. Get this straightened out.

Bones steps further into the room as Chili turns his back on Bones, walks to the sofa and sits down.

CHILI: How'd you get in here?

BONES: I told them I was you. I acted stupid and they believed me.

CHILI: So what brings you to L.A., Bones?

BONES: Don't insult me. Get up and turn around.

Chili gets to his feet. Bones motions with the gun and he turns to face the painting over the sofa. Bones comes over and lifts his wallet from his back pocket.

BONES: You're the dumbest fucking guy I ever met in my life. Let's see what's in your pockets.

His face still to the wall, Chili shoves his hands in and pulls the side pockets out. Bones turns away.

BONES: What you should've done was told me about Leo Devoe as soon as you found out.

Chili looks over his shoulder to see Bones pulling his suitcoat from the back of the chair . . .

CHILI: Why would I do that?

BONES: 'Cause the guy's a customer now, stupid. His ass belongs to me.

Bones lays the pistol on the counter, holds the suitcoat with one hand and feels through it with the other . . . his expression changes, his eyes open wider.

BONES: What have we here?

His hand comes out of the suitcoat with the LOCKER KEY. Chili sits down on the sofa again; he can't believe how easy this is gonna be . . .

CHILI: Give me my cigarettes. They're in the inside pocket.

Bones throws him the coat.

BONES: Help yourself.

Bones then holds up the key to look at it.

BONES: C-one-eight.

Frowning now. Putting on a show.

BONES: I wonder what this's for, a locker? Yeah, but where is it?

Chili sits back to smoke his cigarette, lets it happen.

CHILI: I checked the bag at the airport, when I came.

BONES: Yeah? Which terminal?

CHILI: *(beat)* Sovereign.

BONES: You found Leo, didn't you? Took the poor asshole's money and put it in a locker, ready to go.

(looks at him)

Why haven't you left?

CHILI: I like it here.

Chili shrugs. Bones eyes the key a moment, then . . .

BONES: Look, there's no reason you and I shouldn't get along. Forget all the bullshit from before – I don't even remember how it started. You took a swing at me over some fuckin' thing, whatever it was – forget it. You owe me some money, right? Forget that too. But, you don't say a fuckin' word about this to anybody. It's strictly between you and me, right?

CHILI: Whatever you want, Ray.

EXT. SUNSET MARQUIS HOTEL – NIGHT

As Ray Bones gets into a cab . . .

WOMAN: *(V.O.)* Drug Enforcement Agency.

INT. CHILI'S HOTEL ROOM – LATER

Chili is on the telephone.

CHILI: I wanna speak to the agent in charge.

WOMAN: *(PHONE)* What is this in regard to?

CHILI: A locker out at the airport, full of money.

Chili waits. Then . . .

MAN'S VOICE: *(PHONE)* Who's speaking please?

CHILI: I can't tell you. It's an anonymous call.

MAN: *(PHONE)* Are you the same anonymous asshole called the other day?

CHILI: No, this is a different one. Have you looked in that locker, C-one-eight?

There's a pause on the line.

MAN: You're helping us out. I'd like to know who this is.

CHILI: I bet you would. You want to chat or you want me to tell you who to look for? The guy's on his way out there right now.

MAN: You know there's a reward for information that leads to a conviction. That's why I have to know who this is.

CHILI: I'll get my reward in heaven. The guy you want has a bullet scar in his head and is wearing gray shoes. You can't miss him.

EXT. SUNSET MARQUIS – NIGHT

As Chili follows the bellboy out of the hotel. He tips the guy, then gets in the car with Karen.

KAREN: What took you so long?

CHILI: Couldn't find my toothbrush.

He kisses her, then starts the car.

EXT. SOVEREIGN TERMINAL – LAX – NIGHT

As Bones, seen only from the back now, gets out of the

cab, enters the terminal.

INT. SOVEREIGN TERMINAL – SAME TIME

As Ray Bones, still seen only from the back casually strolls through the terminal, playing with the LOCKER KEY in his hand.

Ray walks right up to C-18 and inserts the key, turns it, and opens the locker to reveal a BLACK ATHLETIC BAG sitting inside . . . Chuckling, he then reaches inside . . .

. . . then stiffens as we hear A CLICK as a RED LASER DOT hits him in the temple . . .

VOICE: Look at me, Boots.

Bones turns his head and we see that it's not the Ray Bones we know, but . . . AN ACTOR, a tough-looking guy with a scary face . . .

WE PULL BACK FURTHER TO REVEAL:

MARTIN WEIR standing there with the biggest fucking gun with laser scope we've ever seen. A BEAUTIFUL WOMAN with the biggest – well, you get the idea – is standing next to him . . . She screams . . .

WOMAN: Watch it, Steve!

Bullets and blood fly as the tough guy pulls a gun from the locker and begins firing wildly at Martin and the Woman and Hare Khrishna's and anybody else who happens to be in the vicinity . . .

Martin, the tough guy only two feet away, calmly aims his

gun and pulls the trigger, but nothing happens. He shakes the gun . . .

MARTIN: Dammit . . . not again . . .

DIRECTOR: Cut!

PULL BACK FARTHER TO REVEAL: A SOUNDSTAGE

Set up like the airport terminal. Martin throws a fit about the malfunctioning prop as The Bear walks up to him.

BEAR: Martin, maybe you should dive or roll out of the way or something . . .

HARRY: Alright, let's wrap! We'll pick it up tomorrow!

As Karen crosses the soundstage, we track along the backs of a row of director's chairs with the names . . . MARTIN WEIR . . . HARRY ZIMM . . . KAREN FLORES AND . . . CHILI PALMER. Chili stands chatting with BUDDY LAFKIN.

BUDDY: But Martin already told me he loves it.

CHILI: Look, I don't know, Buddy, I don't think Martin's right for this new one.

BUDDY: Why the hell not?

CHILI: He's too short.

EXT. SOUNDSTAGE – DUSK

As Karen, Chili, Harry, Martin, and Buddy all exit the soundstage. Karen and Chili get into Chili's minivan.

As they pull out, we see the name 'C. Palmer' painted in the space.

We then CRANE UP AND BACK as Harry, Martin, and Buddy each get into their own minivans . . . and we then . . .

FADE OUT.

BARB WIRE™

Stars the hugely popular Pamela Anderson
of **Baywatch** fame

Based on the highly successful comic
book series

Set in the future in the midst of a postmodern
civil war

Barb Wire, the hard-living bounty hunter finds
herself recruited to aid the escape of a
shadowy Resistance figure

Barb must combat diverse and colourful
forces of evil if there is to be any hope for
world peace

Publication to tie in with major Universal movie

**Boxtree are publishing two
official tie ins to the film –**

**Barb Wire – The Novelisation
0 7522 0199 9, £4.99 pb**

**Barb Wire – Official Fanbook
0 7522 0194 8, £7.99 pb**

FILM TIE INS ORDER FORM

☐ 0 7522 0664 8	Apollo 13, Making of	£8.99 pb
☐ 0 7522 0194 8	Barb Wire – Fan Book	£7.99 pb
☐ 0 7522 0199 9	Barb Wire – Novelisation	£4.99 pb
☐ 0 7522 0694 X	First Knight	£4.99 pb
☐ 1 85283 484 6	Making of GoldenEye	£8.99 pb
☐ 0 7522 0648 6	Murder in the First	£4.99 pb
☐ 0 7522 0138 7	The Net	£4.99 pb
☐ 0 7522 0617 6	Pret a Porter	£16.99 pb
☐ 0 7522 0886 1	Solitaire for Two	£5.99 pb
☐ 0 7522 0211 1	12 Monkeys	£4.99 pb

All these books are available at your local bookshop or can be ordered direct from the publisher. Just tick the titles you want and fill in the form below.

Prices and availability subject to change without notice.

Boxtree Cash Sales, P.O. Box 11, Falmouth, Cornwall TR10 9EN

Please send a cheque or postal order for the value of the book and add the following for postage and packing:

U.K. including B.F.P.O. – £1.00 for one book plus 50p for the second book, and 30p for each additional book ordered up to a £3.00 maximum.

Overseas including Eire – £2.00 for the first book plus £1.00 for the second book, and 50p for each additional book ordered.

OR please debit this amount from my Access/Visa Card (delete as appropriate).

Card Number ☐☐☐☐☐☐☐☐☐☐☐☐☐☐☐☐☐☐

Amount £ ....

Expiry Date ....

Signed ....

Name ....

Address ....

....

....